THE LANGUAGE OF RIDDLES

THE LANGUAGE OF RIDDLES

New Perspectives

W. J. Pepicello
and Thomas A. Green

OHIO STATE UNIVERSITY PRESS : COLUMBUS

Library of Congress Cataloging in Publication Data

Pepicello, W. J., 1949-
The language of riddles.
Bibliography: p.
Includes index.
1. Riddles—History and criticism. I. Green, Thomas A., 1944-
II. Title.
PN6367.P4 1984 398′.6 84-3551

ISBN: 978-0-8142-5345-8

CONTENTS

INTRODUCTION

THIS WORK IS THE RESULT of a long association between the authors, stemming originally from a seminar on folklore and language conducted by Tom Green in 1976. It is based in part on a series of articles that emanated from that seminar (Green and Pepicello 1978, 1979, 1980; Pepicello 1980). Since our initial collaboration, we have beseiged meetings of folklore and linguistic societies, as well as professional journals, with our integrations of folklore and linguistics, striving to establish a focus that both disciplines would find compatible. In so doing, we have found it necessary to present some basic material from both fields, so that the foundations of our analyses are clear to both folklorists and linguists. Our progress toward that goal has been aided immeasurably by discussions with colleagues too numerous to name, as well as by observations and contributions of riddles by students, friends, and passers-by.

Special thanks are due to Dan Ben-Amos, who has provided support and criticism over a period of years. Our thanks also to Roger D. Abrahams and David Stanley for providing many examples and comments that have proven useful and enlightening. Of course, we alone are responsible for our analyses. Our gratitude goes also to Melanie Gross, whose typing efforts were above and beyond the call of duty. Finally, our deepest appreciation goes to our wives, who have been the willing victims of countless riddles through several versions of this work.

The order of authors' names is not significant.

LANGUAGE AND ART IN RIDDLES

Chapter One

IN THE FOLLOWING PAGES, we hope to offer new perspectives on the riddle in its enactment both as a conventional use of ordinary language and as an art form. Such an approach involves paying constant attention to the utilitarian, objective aspects of conventional speech on the one hand, and the more emotive, subjective aspects inherent in the artful performance of a folk genre on the other hand (see Guiraud 1971: 10–11). Although the separation of art and language may seem somewhat artificial, the riddle foregrounds linguistic code as well as aesthetic convention in its performance. Lucid 1977 in a critique of Lotman 1970 neatly characterizes this interplay of language and art: "The model of external communication consists of a code and a message that is encoded, transmitted and decoded. In contrast, the scheme of internal communication posits an initial code and the transformation of the message. . . . Art arises within internal speech as an antithesis to the practical speech of external messages but oscillates . . . between these two modes of communication" (Lucid 1977:11). Thus, the realization of an art form requires a subjective, internal perception to be transformed into a code from which receivers (an audience) can derive a meaning. Art is not free to innovate, but is subjected to semiotic constraints, those of some primary code (graphic, aural).

Though still semiotic, aesthetic constraints (artistic conventions) are of a different order, a secondary system imposed on the primary code. This set of constraints proves to be crucial to the realization of artful constructs, also. It is the case, as asserted in Uspensky 1977, that "Every work of art is conventional, for it always presupposes some norm as the background against which it is perceived" (1977:172). Art, then, can hardly be conceived of as novel in any genuine sense of that word. It simply provides a mode for the reexamination of phenomena in terms of a finite set of conventions. This set of conventions may be expanded by a variety of means (some of which are described in this study), but at any given time the artistic expression is compelled to operate within a preestablished cultural framework. The boundaries within which art can operate are suggested by the following remarks found in Edie 1976: "Once men have culturally organized their experience in a distinctive manner, and chosen their metaphors, they tend to think within the cultural-linguistic bounds that they have unwittingly set for themselves. They no longer think as they *will* but as they *can*" (1976:170). Such conventional constraints on art in general are especially intense in traditional expressive culture.

We find then that our form-breaking techniques are limited aesthetically by cultural convention; similarly, they are limited linguistically by grammatical convention, and it is here that the focus of our study is to be found. For despite the constraints, within the limits just discussed we may explore linguistic and aesthetic structures, highlighting our knowledge of and facility with these structures. Thus, such notions as reclassification or inversion in riddling should not be taken to mean that riddles contain original metaphors or establish new linguistic epistemologies; rather, riddles play upon a common cultural repertoire of traditional categories, both linguistic and aesthetic, which are subjected to playful manipulation, but never demolished, on riddling occasions. Thus we see the riddle genre as employing organizing principles within a conventional framework.

Yet clearly riddles obscure a message, as well as the code, i.e., the limits on the forms that a message may take. In the artful manipulation of linguistic and aesthetic codes, we may find an affirmation of the cultural convention, the message, which is hidden in the riddle form. But if riddles are indeed conventional, we might well ask how they achieve their artful end. We shall contend that the essential element in this regard is context, both linguistic and cultural. That is, the contextual frame for riddling is one of performance, as opposed to the normal communicative frame in utilitarian speech. The latter is highly contextualized, and its goal is to facilitate the flow of information; the former suspends normal context, and its goal is to impede the flow of information for the purpose of outwitting the riddlee.

Thus the interplay of code, message, and context is central to our discussion of the riddle, and we shall consider each element in turn. First, however, we need to address the framework within which this interplay occurs, namely that of performance. For if riddling employs organizing principles, as we have claimed, those principles come from the licensed performance of riddles. It is the performance of riddles that enables us to discuss more fully the personal, social, and aesthetic patterns they reveal. The license to exploit such patterns is basic to our analysis; therefore, let us treat this matter more fully.

Performance in contemporary folklore studies, as suggested by Bauman 1975, conveys "a dual sense of artistic *action*—the doing of folklore—and artistic *event*—the performance situation, involving performer, art form, audience, and setting" (1975:290). Although the bulk of the work on performance has been done only recently, folklore's concern with performance predates the recent flurry of activity.

Jansen 1957 argues that there is a "need for notes about the conditions of the actual performance" (1957:10) and indicates that the concern with the performance of folk materials predates his own essay by 25 years, although no specific works are cited in this regard. Jansen suggests that the term *performance* must be employed in its theatrical sense, for he notes that the presentation of an item of folklore requires the performer to assume "a pose toward his audience . . . that differs from his everyday, every-hour-in-theday relationship to that same audience" (1957:112–13). Jansen's image of folk performer as actor, in a sense, anticipates conclusions drawn by more recent theorists, e.g., Abrahams 1968 and Goffman 1974.

Jansen, however, does not regard performance as a primary object for study, since he explicitly states, "The folklorist is, and must be, primarily concerned with the content, the material of folklore" (1957:111). Moreover, whereas contemporary scholars with an interest in performance tend to regard verbal folklore as, by definition, performance, he views it as a quantifiable element. Thus, he regards performance as something different from Bauman's "doing." It is, rather, discussed in terms of the abandonment of mundane social roles and the entry, to a greater or lesser degree, into the alternative role of performer (or "poser" in Jansen's terminology). Although he does not touch on the important issue of ongoing influences during performance, Jansen does point out the utility of dealing with performance context (the situation surrounding the rendering) as well as texts (the "script" of a particular rendering) when addressing questions of function.

With the call of Hymes 1970 for an ethnography of speaking that would be "concerned with the situation and uses, the patterns and functions, of speaking as an activity in its own right" (1970:101), many of those scholars with an interest in the performance of traditional aesthetic products saw the utility of perceiving folklore as a way of speaking governed by specific rules and subject to all the cross-cultural variations of speech. Two distinguished efforts in this area are the discussion of proverbs as culture-specific communication in Arewa and Dundes 1964 and the analysis of the emergent nature of performance during storytelling events in Georges 1969.

Although there is general agreement among those folklorists who focus on performance as a central concept of the discipline, individual formulations of and approaches to the materials are subject to variation. To illustrate, Lomax 1968 argues that in the social organization of the singing group is to be found "the key to understanding the performance situation . . . and its relationship to social structures" (1968:155). Thus, in Lomax' opinion, the analysis of performance events provides the key to unlocking submerged sociocultural patterns. Abrahams 1968, seeking a method that would take into account performance, item, and audience, draws on the insights provided by the contextual interests of the functionalist school of anthropology and the structural concerns of modern literary critics (especially Kenneth Burke) in order to study the "organizational elements of both items and performance" (1968:145). More recently Abrahams (ms.) has characterized performance as the coming together of an occasion, a performer, a performance tradition (i.e., the past experience of the group on similar occasions), and an audience capable of observing and judging effectively. He clearly deals with the constraints in performance events that keep innovation within acceptable frameworks for folk audiences. Ben-Amos 1971, in another reaction against earlier textually-oriented approaches to folklore, argues, "There is no dichotomy between processes and products. The telling is the tale; therefore the narrator, his story, and his audience are all related to each other as components of a single continuum, which is the communicative event" (1971:10).

In spite of minor differences in emphasis, then, the perspectives of performance theorists converge in the assertion that it is crucial to discuss verbal folklore as rule-governed utterance *in situ* that exploits traditional organizational patterns rather than as text in isolation; however, it remains a unique rendering within certain circumscribed boundaries. Such a convergence of approaches, as argued by Geertz, allows for an interdisciplinary "unpacking of performed meaning" (1980:174). Our aim is to unpack a number of the linguistic layers of riddle performance, thereby delineating another set of boundaries within which the witty devices of riddles are employed.

Goffman 1974 deals not only with the boundaries discussed by Abrahams and Ben-Amos, but adds another dimension in his assertion that "A performance . . . is that arrangement which transforms an individual into a stage performer, the latter, in turn, being an object that can be looked at in the round and at length without offense, and looked to for engaging behavior, by persons in an 'audience' role" (1974:124). Goffman's notion of transformation emphasizes another element of the performance event in noting that at some point the performer must act, not only in a special role, but to signal his entry into a circumscribed realm or be in danger of social censure because of his manipulation of basic conventions of reference. In order to discuss this realm and the products that arise from it, the idea of a "frame" explicated by Bateson 1972 has been adopted by Goffman, as well as by scholars from a variety of disciplines.

According to Bateson, the frame is a set of implicit or explicit messages providing clues for the interpretation of coexistent messages; the former in Bateson's terminology are "metamessages" (i.e., messages about messages). The importance of this principle in the present discussion is that the use of these metamessages is to transform organizational patterns appropriate to serious behavior into ludic actions. Our sporting contests provide a number of illustrations of these principles in operation. For example, the metamessages of a boxing match (a restricted playing area, a referee, judges, and special protective equipment) that coexist with very real blows, cause us to interpret this activity as a game rather than as an actual fight. In the case of verbal interaction, there are also elements that serve as framing devices that are culturally recognized transformers of speech from talk into performance. Bauman 1975:295 cites several examples:

1. special codes, e.g., archaic or esoteric language, reserved for and diagnostic of performance (e.g., Toelken 1969, Sherzer 1974);

2. special formulae that signal performance, such as conventional openings and closings, or explicit statements announcing or asserting performance (e.g., Crowley 1966, Reaver 1972, Uspensky 1972, Babcock-Abrahams 1974);

3. figurative language, such as metaphor, metonymy, etc. (e.g., Keenan 1973, 1974, Fox 1974, Rosaldo 1973, Sherzer 1974);

4. formal stylistic devices, such as rhyme, vowel harmony, other forms of parallelism (Jakobson 1966, 1968, Stankiewicz 1960, Austerlitz 1960, Gossen 1972, 1974, Fox 1974, Sherzer and Sherzer 1972);

5. special prosodic patterns of tempo, stress, pitch (e.g., Lord 1960, Tedlock 1972);

6. special paralinguistic patterns of voice quality and vocalization (e.g., Tedlock 1972, McDowell 1974);

7. appeal of tradition (e.g., Innes 1974);

8. disclaimer of performance (e.g., Darnell 1974, Keenan 1974).

By means of such conventional devices, the aesthetic tradition of each group provides its performers with the means for framing verbal art, for signaling the audience to a performance event that what co-occurs with such devices is somehow different from what has come before and what will be presented in the stream of utterance to follow. What emerges from this reorientation is a move from the traditional text into the heart of such structures, the group expectations surrounding their forms and performances—aesthetic conventions, and the ways in which these play upon nonludic formulae.

It is with these conventions, specifically the conventions of description, that this study intends to deal. For our material, we rely in large measure on English-speaking traditions and remain within Western culture. Our data are drawn from published collections, our own field work, and those field notes colleagues have generously provided. Despite the limitations of this corpus, the arguments based upon it appear generally applicable to the riddle genre in a variety of cultural contexts. Moreover, as is suggested in the final pages of this study, our arguments concerning riddles apply to other traditional art forms as well.

In our examination of the structure of riddles, we must remember that they, like all art, provide conventional yet creative means by which principles of order are rehearsed and revealed (cf. Abrahams, 1972:177). Applying our original paradox to our current problem, it is clear that for the riddle to work it must encompass both innovation (creativity) and convention as they emerge in performance. This difficult task is accomplished by manipulating the code(s) involved to create striking images without departing from the parameters provided by these accepted frameworks. Our arguments are based on the realization that riddles may bring perceptions into "saying" but not into "being." They simply exploit preexisting patterns of various sorts. The conventional patterns exploited in riddles are drawn from at least two interrelated systems: the linguistic and the aesthetic.

The linguistic system of any group imposes the most formal set of constraints on its verbal art forms. Despite flexible areas, the grammar of any natural language limits the range of deviation within which communication can be accomplished. In its most general terms, a language, or any communicative system for that matter, must provide a code by which, as Lotman 1970 observed, messages can be encoded, transmitted, and decoded by those with whom we wish to communicate. Such systems require a high degree of predictability attainable only through relative rigidity.

It is in aesthetic systems that the group's unique organizational formats are expressed through symbolic means. As Burke 1968 notes, "The forms of art . . . are not exclusively 'aesthetic.' They can be said to have a prior existence in the experiences of the person hearing or reading the work of art. They parallel processes which characterize his experiences outside of art" (1968:143). Thus our traditional verbal art should be seen in relation to other patterns of experience established in the performing group.

As regards riddling the influences of shared aesthetic-cultural patterns have been recognized for some time (e.g., Hamnett 1967 and Abrahams 1972). Verbal art emerges, then, in the interaction of the linguistically permissible with the aesthetically desirable. Moreover, both sets of constraints are closely related to other sociocultural organizational patterns of the group. Within such restrictions, how can novel perception be created?

Emotive ends (i.e., deviation from a narrowly referential transfer of information) may be achieved because our communicative systems are not constructed of impermeable categories. Our systems invariably "leak." These "leaks," more properly areas of flexibility in the code, are what lead to occasional misunderstandings concerning the nature and interpretation of a message. More importantly, however, these resilient areas are often consciously exploited. Such exploitation occurs even outside the circumscribed realm of art. Linguistic change, for example, could not occur in the absence of such a system. "Human languages," Thomas 1969 writes, "are noticeably redundant . . . we use more elements than are needed to convey our meaning. This fact contributes to linguistic flexibility. The flexibility, in turn, facilitates linguistic change" (1969:34–35). Our concern, however, is with the exploitation of these flexible areas in performance contexts.

As we have previously noted, with the appearance of signals that ongoing activity constitutes performance as opposed to mere behavior, a special interpretative frame that contrasts with the literal is called into being. Behavior that ordinarily would be labeled inept or even overtly antisocial is frequently permitted and, in fact, encouraged in performance situations. The influential arguments found in Bateson 1972 demonstrate that the signals that "this is play" allow for the manipulation of the orders and disorders of nonludic experience without censure. Under such circumstances those patterns that are ordinarily interpreted as violations or incompetence may become virtuosity if they demonstrate intentionality. Even clumsiness may become art if it is manifestly intentional; if, in Kenneth Burke's terms, it is an *act*: "As for 'act,' any verb no matter how specific or how general, that has connotations of consciousness of purpose falls under this category. If one happened to stumble over an obstruction, that would not be an act, but mere motion.

However, one could convert even this sheer accident into something if, in the course of falling, one suddenly *willed* his fall" (Burke 1969:14).

It would be unwise in delineating the qualities of verbal art (though perhaps not impossible) to regard as artful an *in medias res* conversion from action to act, but Burke is correct in calling our attention to the principle of intentionality as the central criterion for separating art from simple behavior. The following comment on metaphor by Gardner and colleagues 1978 reinforces Burke's argument: "To qualify as metaphor . . . the link formed must be *intentional* and *conscious*, rather than accidental or inadvertent" (1978:6). The "link" we attend to in metaphor is the coupling of a term's "original" sense with a novel usage in performance (in the previously discussed folkloristic rather than the Chomskyan linguistic sense of this term). As commentators from Aristotle (*The Poetics*) to the present (cf. Gardner and colleagues 1978:15) have argued, in metaphor a renaming occurs. However, there is not mere substitution, but an overlapping of frames of reference for lexical items and phrases. As Edie 1976 characterizes the situation, "A word can become a metaphor, take on a new sense, only because, and precisely because it can enable us to *take it as something else* without ceasing thereby to signify its own original meaning" (1976:187).

Thus, tensions of various sorts (Gardner and colleagues 1978:6 notes the tensions between original and changed metaphorical meanings) are purposely generated in performance: literal meaning vs. metaphorical meaning, accident vs. intention, utilitarian vs. ludic, to name but a few. In verbal art this is possible only because language is systematic; it constitutes a pattern that although followed in utilitarian communications, may be subverted in play. As Thomas 1969 states concerning metaphor, although the same could be said of all verbal art, "If there were no system . . . then there could be no novelty" (1969:35).

In riddles the system of language employed by the folk group may be subverted in various ways through the intentional overlapping of frames of reference for purposes of temporarily blocking communication. These means will be given detailed treatment in subsequent chapters. Let us begin to indicate the two major devices at this juncture, however.

The first, linguistic ambiguity, involves single utterances that may yield multiple semantic interpretations. Linguistic ambiguity arises when words are used in their literal senses; there is no recourse to the creative renaming that typifies figurative language. The following example is representative.

John hit the lady with the blue umbrella.

This utterance is subject to two readings: (1) John employed a blue umbrella as an instrument to strike a certain woman, or (2) John struck a woman who is identified by the fact that she carries a blue umbrella. Both interpretations are appropriate and both are literal. Two underlying semantic structures are represented by a single utterance. These structures do not rely on any novel reshaping of preexisting systems.

If we may assume that utilitarian speech strives for clarity (and it must to achieve its referential goals efficiently), we conclude such overlap is assiduously avoided outside playful contexts. There are various means, primarily contextual, by which we attempt to prevent ambiguous utterance. When such slips do occur in utilitarian speech, we regard them as accidents caused by the inherent flexibility of the code. In riddling, however, we exploit these accidents, and if successful, the riddler is credited with wit rather than incompetence.

Similarly, metaphor, though nonliteral, depends on the ability of language to create multiple frames of reference. By the same token, novel metaphor (as opposed to idiom, i.e., "frozen metaphor") may be dangerous in that meaning is not readily apparent. Its dangers in utilitarian speech result in its usefulness to verbal play, especially the riddle genre, in which the blocking of direct transfer of information is the ideal.

We shall begin our examination of riddles as verbal art from a linguistic perspective and build toward a characterization of the genre as an integration of formal linguistic and culturally aesthetic strategies. For regardless of the device used to create a block in riddles, for example, conventional tropes or syntactic ambiguity, the form is grounded in language. We therefore take the structure of English as our base upon which to construct our comments about the riddle genre. We take the linguistic domain of the riddle to encompass the grammar of a language, in this case English. We shall approach language as a system consisting of basically three levels: (1) a level of sound or utterance, phonology; (2) a level of word-formation, morphology; and (3) a level of sentence formation, syntax. Semantics, the meaning component of language, will be assumed to permeate all levels and will be dealt with in like manner.[1]

At the level of phonology, we are concerned with the distinctive sounds of English, i.e., those sounds that native speakers perceive as basic units of language for purposes of communication. For instance, if we consider the pronunciation of the pair of words *bet* and *pet*, we find that speakers of English uniformly recognize the pair as consisting of two words with different meanings. Since the final sequence of vowel plus consonant is identical in the two words (i.e., they rhyme), the distinguishing factor must be in the initial consonants. On closer examination of the initial consonants, we find that both "p" and "b" are articulated by pursing the lips and then releasing a slight puff of air while unpursing the lips. We call this a *bilabial* articulation. We notice one difference between the two sounds, however: in the articulation of "b," we notice that the vocal cords are vibrating; this is not true in the articulation of "p." Thus, if the distinction between *pet* and *bet* rests on the differentiation of "p" and "b," we find that this differentiation is in the state of the vocal cords during the bilabial articulation. Since this differentiation of "p" and "b" is functional in English in that it serves in determining the identities of different words, it is distinctive and must be taken into account in the description of the English language.

Furthermore, since we shall be concerned in this study primarily with actual speech, in the form of orally transmitted riddles, we must employ a system of notation in which each distinctive sound of English has one and only one symbol which identifies that sound. In this way we level out spelling problems, such as the "f" sounds of *fish*, *philosophy*, and *enough*, by representing this sound everywhere as /f/. A list of phonemic symbols appears on page 19.

At the level of word formation, we are concerned with the combination of distinctive units of sound (phonemes) into meaningful grammatical units, which we call morphemes. Consider, for example, the English word *discontinues*, a third-person singular, present-tense verb. This "word" consists of three morphemes: a negative prefix *dis–*; a basic root *continue*; and a person-tense marker for verbs, the suffix *–s*. We can represent this morphological analysis using phonemic notation (always indicated by slashes), as /dIs - kən-tInyu - z/. Again we see the value in divorcing ourselves from spelling in that the third-person singular, present-tense marker, which is written with a "s," is in fact pronounced in this case /z/.

At the level of sentence formation, or syntax, we are concerned primarily with defining the underlying, or conceptual, structure of an utterance and relating this conceptual structure to the actual utterance itself, which we call the surface structure. That is, given an utterance like:

1. Alex wants to go.

we are concerned first with what the underlying propositions of this utterance are. In this case, there are two:

2. Alex wants something.
3. Alex goes.

Once we have determined the underlying propositions, we need to determine the syntactic relationship between them. That is, we need to be able to formally represent the fact that proposition 3 is the object of proposition 2. We do this in generative-transformational theory by means of a "tree notation" known as phrase structure, which is simply a system for representing the underlying syntactic relationships of utterances like 1. A tree for sentence 1 would look roughly like figure 1. We see here that S_1 (where S means "clause") contains a subject noun phrase (NP) and a verb phrase (VP). The subject NP consists of a noun (N), *Alex*. The VP

Figure 1

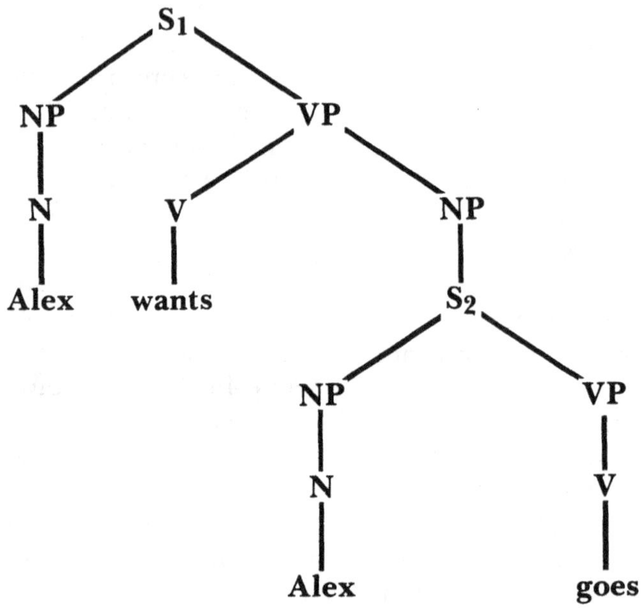

consists of a verb (V) and an object NP, which in this case is another S. Thus, we have formalized our intuitions about the underlying propositions of 1 and their syntactic relationship.

We need next to concern ourselves with how the surface structure seen in 1 is derived from the underlying structure in figure 1. To accomplish this, it is necessary that certain processes be applied to the underlying structure. The cumulative effect of these processes is to yield the surface structure. These processes we call transformations. In the case of the underlying structure in figure 1, the most obvious difference between it and its corresponding surface structure is that the N *Alex* appears twice in the underlying structure but only once in the surface structure. Therefore, one of the occurrences of *Alex*, the one in S_2, must be deleted. This is done by a transformation called Equivalent NP Deletion, which states that with certain verbs (like *want*, *beg*, *refuse*), if the subject of the object clause is the same as the subject of the main clause, then the subject of the object clause may be deleted. Thus, after the application of Equivalent NP Deletion, figure 1 would look like figure 2. Now, since the verb in S_2, *goes*, has no subject with which to agree, it becomes a nonfinite verb form, i.e., an infinitive, *to go*. Application of a subject-verb agreement rule in S_1 then yields the desired utterance *Alex wants to go*.

This example is intended only as an introduction to the type of syntactic analysis we shall develop throughout this work. Although descriptions of underlying structures and transformations will be treated and explained individually, it is important here to characterize the relationship of underlying to surface structure. Underlying structure is designed to formally represent a level of grammar that native speakers recognize intuitively. In this way it formalizes relationships that may not always be obvious in surface structure

Figure 2

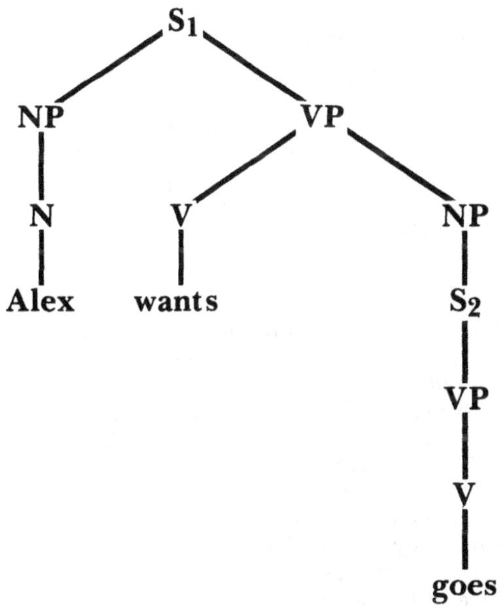

(i.e., the actual utterance), but that the native speaker knows exist, nevertheless. This native speaker intuition we call *competence*. Surface structure, on the other hand, is a representation of an utterance as it is actually produced in speech. It includes all of the imperfections (e.g., slips of the tongue, false starts, unintentional ambiguity) associated with normal speech. This actualization of underlying structure we call *performance*. Generative-transformational grammar, then, seeks to relate competence to performance through the formal devices of underlying structures, transformations, and surface structures.

It is the concern of linguistics to characterize utterances from their inception in thought (semantics) to their realizations in sound. With the formalisms of phonology, morphology, and syntax, we can do this in an ordered manner. For in order to communicate any idea, we must be able to put the idea into a form that is recognizable to those with whom we wish to communicate. This formal, conventional form we call the grammar of language. It entails the use of various combinations of morphemes to represent concepts and the use of syntax to express the relationships between these concepts. Once we have encoded our idea, we then need to transmit it. The medium of speech is sound, and the actualization of the encoded message is in units of distinctive sound, phonemes. It is this system, then, that we will explore insofar as it may be exploited in the riddle genre.

1. Much of the analysis to be proposed is tied to linguistic theory. For purposes of clarity and simplicity, we employ a basically structural approach to phonology and morphology similar to that found in Francis 1958. Our treatment of syntactic phenomena is based on the generative-transformational model initiated in Chomsky 1957 and 1965. The aspects of these works that we employ in our analysis are those we find most useful in bringing new light to bear on the riddle genre. Our analysis is not tied exclusively to these theories, however, and could be formulated within the framework of other current theories of language. Such alternative analyses, and the theoretical issues they involve, are beyond the scope of this work.

Phonemic Symbols

Symbol	*Example*	*Symbol*	*Example*
/p/	pat	/iy/	beet
/b/	bat	/I/	bit
/t/	tip	/ey/	bait
/d/	dip	/ɛ/	bet
/k/	cab	/æ/	bat
/g/	gab	/uw/	boot
/f/	fine	/ʊ/	book
/v/	vine	/ow/	boat
/θ/	thin	/ɔ/	(caught)
/ð/	then	/ɐ/	(bottle)
/s/	sip	/a/	father
/z/	zip	/ə/	sofa, but
/h/	hip	/oy/	boy
/š/	ship	/aw/	cow
/ž/	beige	/ay/	buy
/č/	church		
/ǰ/	judge		
/m/	map		
/n/	nap		
/ŋ/	ring		
/l/	lip		
/r/	rip		
/w/	wet		
/y/	yet		

AMBIGUITY AND WIT

Chapter Two

WE TURN NOW TO our analysis of the riddle as language. Our point of departure for this analysis will be an examination of wit and ambiguity in riddles. For it seems that a basic problem in the consideration of the riddle is that the riddlee is (or should be) incapable of solving riddles posed by the riddler. That is, there is a block element (see p. 73), or what appears to be unsolvable opposition, contained within the composition of the riddle. It will be our contention that this block element is directly related to the notion of ambiguity in two senses. First, there is often linguistic ambiguity, i.e., ambiguity in the grammatical form of the riddle. Second, there is contextual ambiguity, i.e., ambiguity produced through a conscious manipulation of social decorum that results in disorientation or confusion of the riddlee, within the riddle act itself. Thus, the riddler attempts to outwit the riddlee by presenting ambiguities that the riddlee cannot resolve. The notion of "wit," or of "being outwitted," then, can be equated with the riddlee's inability to resolve these ambiguities. Our goal is to define the particular aspects of wit that correlate with the two senses of ambiguity we have characterized, as they relate to the riddle.

We shall deal first with the strictly linguistic notion of ambiguity. Ambiguity, in this sense, refers to the situation that obtains in language when two or more different underlying semantic structures may be represented by a single surface structure representation. The nature of this surface representation is such that the actual utterance (i.e., the phonological form) of the ambiguous structure is identical in both or all of its semantic interpretations. However, this correspondence of surface forms may have several sources. That is, this correspondence may be the result of linguistic processes that occur at the phonological, morphological, or syntactic levels of grammar.

To clarify this claim, we shall exemplify these three types of ambiguity in ordinary conversation. In ordinary speech ambiguity is considered to be a linguistic accident, i.e., it is not planned. Such an accident may occur at any of the three levels we have specified. So, for example, consider sentence 1.

1. John lives near the bank.

The ambiguity here lies in the word *bank*, in that it may refer to a building, a mound of earth, or the sloping earth on either side of a river. Such an ambiguity is purely a surface phonological one, in that we are dealing with three separate lexical items that have identical phonological forms, /bæŋk/. These three lexical items are all the same part of speech, nouns, and differ only by semantic features.

This type of ambiguity is to be distinguished from the type exhibited in sentences 2 and 3.

2. The book is red.
3. The book is read.

The phonological forms of these two sentences are identical, with the ambiguity lying in the utterance of the item /rɛd/. But we can see here that the reason for the correspondence of the surface forms is quite different from that of sentence 1. That is, in sentence 1 we had three lexical items, all nouns, with identical phonological forms. In sentences 2 and 3, however, we find that the underlying difference of the two identical surface structures stems from the morphological level of grammar. Thus, in sentence 2 /rɛd/ is a simple lexical item, an adjective. But in sentence 3, the surface form /rɛd/ must be interpreted as the verb /riyd/ plus its past participle morpheme, which in the case of this irregular verb consists of a vowel change from /iy/ to /ɛ/. Therefore, the semantic difference between the identical phonological forms of sentences 2 and 3 is not the result of a mere correspondence of the phonological forms of independent lexical items, but rather of an identity that results from a process of English morphology.

Finally, ambiguity may result from processes that take place at the syntactic level of grammar. Let us consider first sentences like sentence 4.

4. Sam looked over the car.

The ambiguity in sentence 4 rests on the syntactic classification of *over*. For in underlying structure, *over* may function as a preposition that takes a noun object (figure 3), or as a particle which is part of the verb phrase (figure 4).[1] In the former case, sentence 4 indicates an action whereby Sam cast a glance in a manner such that his line of vision was above the level of the car; in the latter case, sentence 4 indicates that Sam studied the car. It is necessary to show that the surface ambiguity of *over* is not merely phonological,

Figure 3

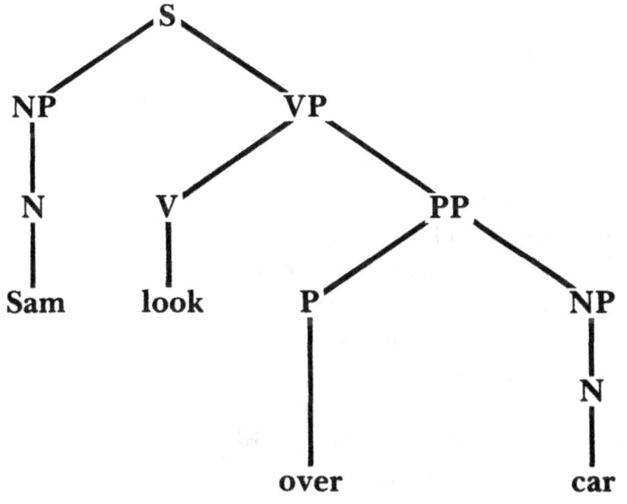

Figure 4

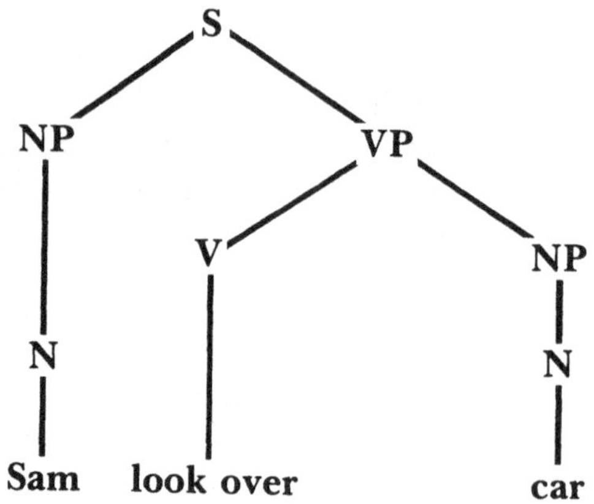

and that the difference in this case is indeed syntactic. This can be shown if we disambiguate sentence 4 in the following way. Notice that it is possible to move the particle "over" to the end of its clause in figure 4, yielding sentence 5.

5. Sam looked the car over.

This sentence is unambiguous and means only that Sam studied the car. That is, sentence 5 cannot have the meaning connected with the underlying structure in figure 3. We see, then, that although the particle "*over*" may be moved to the end of its clause (by a transformation called Particle Movement), the same is not true of the preposition "over." The fact that the lexical items pronounced /owvər/ do not act alike syntactically proves that they are different kinds of syntactic constituents and therefore participate in different kinds of syntactic relationships. This type of syntactic ambiguity, in which two different underlying syntactic constituents have the same phonological form, we call phrase structure ambiguity, since the syntactic difference is revealed in the underlying trees, or phrase structure syntactic configurations of the ambiguous constructions.

Another kind of syntactic ambiguity results when the application of transformations to two different underlying structures results in homophonous surface structures. For example, consider sentence 6.

6. Who do you expect to marry?

This sentence is multiply ambiguous. Let us consider two of the possible readings and their sources of ambiguity. On one reading, sentence 6 is asking about your expectation of another person marrying some unidentified third party (figure 5). On another reading, sentence 6 is asking for the identification of the person with whom you intend to enter into marriage (figure 6).

It is immediately apparent that the underlying structures in figures 5 and 6 are substantially different. However, the nature of the transformation that produces questions in English (called Question Formation) has the effects on both

Figure 5

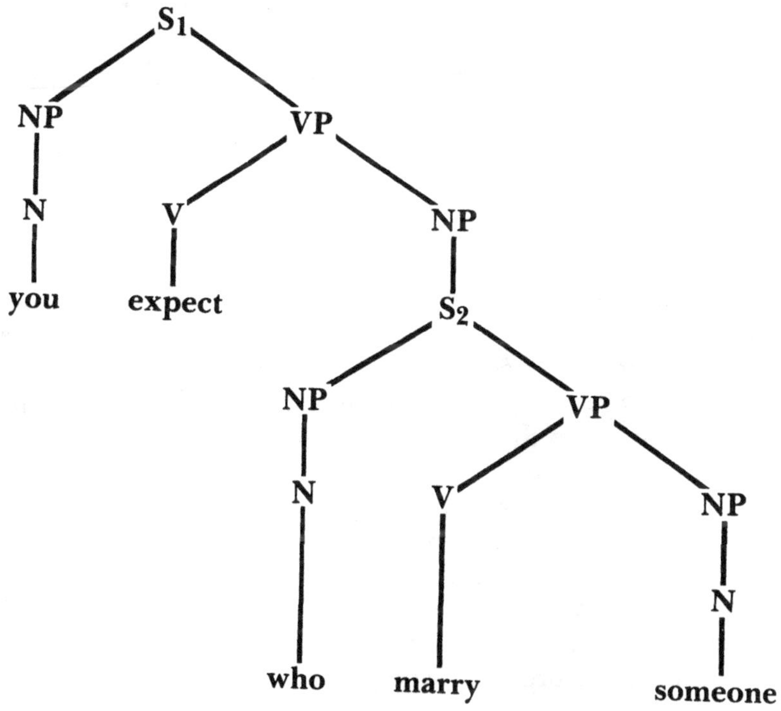

Figure 6

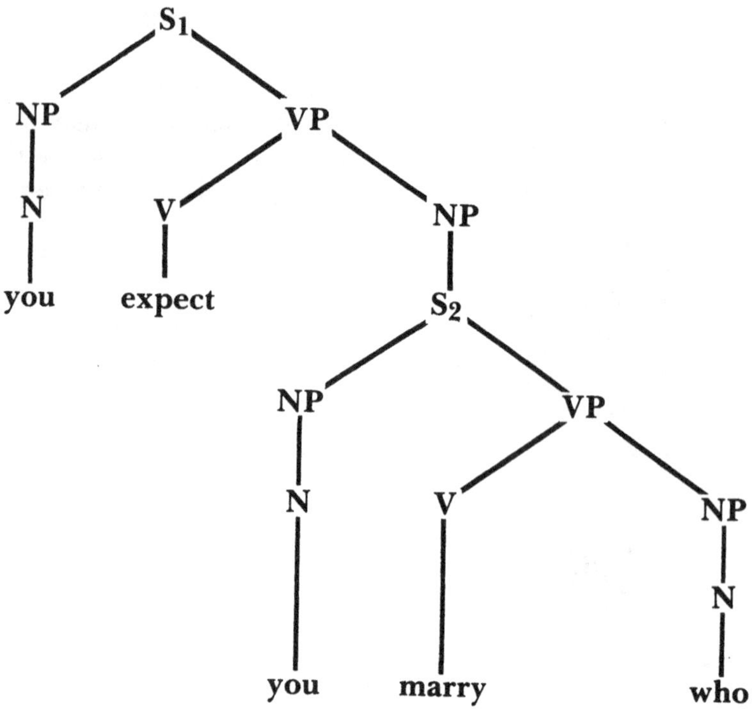

underlying structures of moving the interrogative pronoun "who" to the front of the entire structure. Then in figure 6, a transformation called Unspecified Pronoun Deletion allows the indefinite (i.e., unspecified) pronoun "someone" to be deleted from object position in S_2. The results of these separate derivations are identical, yielding homophonous surface structures of the form in sentence 6.

Thus we see that ambiguity in ordinary speech may have three sources. It should be noticed that we avoid the term *semantic ambiguity*, since in fact all ambiguity is by nature (and definition) semantic. Our concern here has been to explain the grammatical relationships that obtain between underlying (semantic/syntactic) structure and surface (phonological) structure, and which may result in ambiguity.

We proceed now to an examination of how linguistic ambiguity is exploited in the riddle genre to produce wit. That is, we shall explore how these three types of ambiguity, which are considered accidents in ordinary speech, may be consciously manipulated in riddling. We shall see how the riddler, in creating ambiguity in the form of the riddle, has a double advantage. First, only he knows *where* in the composition of the riddle an ambiguity exists. Second, only he knows *at what linguistic level* this ambiguity exists.

In dealing with linguistic ambiguity in the riddle, we note one important consideration for such a study. Since language is, as we have seen, a communication system composed of three subsystems that are designed to actualize semantic information, it is inevitable that these subsystems will interact. That is, a given riddle may simultaneously employ ambiguity at more than one linguistic level. In such cases, it is pointless to debate which level of ambiguity is more basic, since there are no criteria for making such a determination. It is, nevertheless, necessary to note and classify such interactions, since we are concerned with characterizing linguistic aspects of wit in the riddle. Therefore, we shall deal first with each linguistic level in relative isolation, detailing how it may be exploited in riddling. Our secondary concern will be how the interactions of various of the three levels also serve to create ambiguity.

We begin at the phonological level, with an examination of lexical ambiguity in the riddle.[2] There are two basic exploitations of this type of ambiguity, the first of which is seen in riddles like those in sentences 7, 8, and 9.

7. What turns but does not move? *Milk.*
8. What has a mouth but does not eat? *River.*
9. What has an eye but cannot see? *Needle.*

In each of these cases, the ambiguity is caused by the fact that two different lexical items have identical phonological form. Thus, /tərn/, /mawθ/, and /ay/ may each have at least two different referents.

Aside from this possibility of different lexical items having identical phonological form, the underlying structures involved in the various interpretations of the riddle questions in sentences 7, 8, and 9 are identical. For example, the underlying structure of sentence 7 is roughly similar to figure 7. This structure specifies that some indefinite NP performs the action of turning (S_1), but does not perform the action of moving (S_2). That this indefinite NP is the same in both S_1 and S_2 is indicated by the subscript marker $_i$. That the verb in S_2 is negated is indicated by the marker NEG that is attached to S_2. The actual series of transformations that derives the surface question from the underlying structure involves basically three operations. First, the NP "something$_i$" in S_2 can be deleted since it is identical with the NP "something$_i$" in S_1. This transformation is common in English when one NP is the subject of two or more verbs. So, for example, in a sentence such as *Joe likes dogs and Joe likes cats*, we may eliminate the second occurrence of *Joe* (and of *likes*, as well), giving *Joe likes dogs and cats*. The application of this transformation to figure 7 results in a structure like *Something turns but does not move.* The transformation called Question Formation then changes the indefinite NP "some-

Figure 7

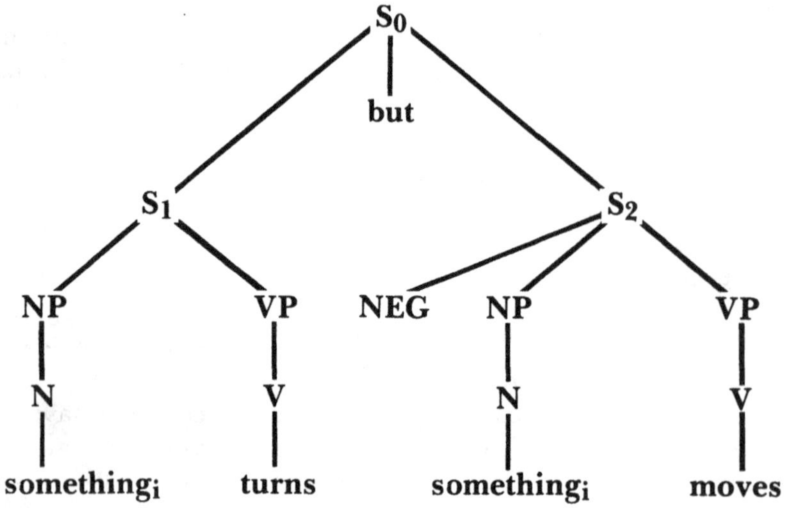

thing" into the corresponding interrogative pronoun, namely "what," yielding the surface question of sentence 7.

Regardless of which semantic interpretation we choose for the lexical item "turn," the syntactic, morphological, and phonological processes involved in forming a question from figure 7 are identical. That is, since the only variable in the differing interpretations of the question in sentence 7 is the semantic marking of the verb "turn," it is here that the ambiguity of sentence 7 is to be found.

Whereas the ambiguity of sentence 7 rests on the interpretation of a verb, that of sentence 8 is to be found in an ambiguous noun. Thus, the underlying structure of sentence 8 is roughly similar to figure 8.

The deletion of identical subject NPs discussed above yields a structure *Something has a mouth but does not eat*, which is transformed into sentence 8 by Question Formation. Here, regardless of which semantic interpretation for *mouth* is chosen, the derivation of the question is exactly the same phonologically, morphologically, and syntactically. The ambi-

Figure 8

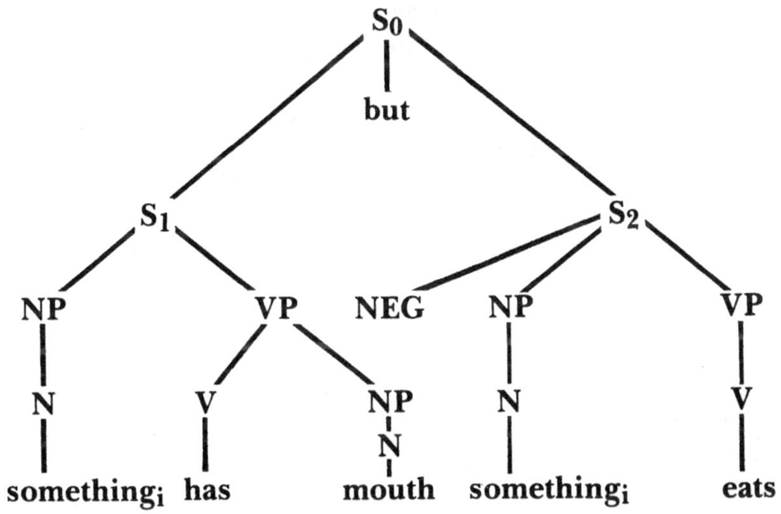

guity therefore lies in the choice of semantic interpretation for the lexical item, a noun, *mouth*.

In these cases, then, it is clear that the ambiguity involved is a result of homophony. That is, the pronunciation of various underlying concepts (i.e., words) is identical. In such cases the advantage of the riddler in posing riddles is that only he knows which semantic interpretation is involved in the riddle, and, indeed, he may demand, in some instances, any of the possible interpretations from the riddles as the correct answer. It should be noticed here that the homophonous constituents are always the same parts of speech, and that the lexical items may or may not be morphemically complex. However, if there is morphemic complexity, there is also a one-to-one homophony of morphemes. Thus in sentence 7, /tərnz/ consists of two morphemes, the root verb /tərn/ and the third person singular present tense morpheme /–z/. Since the ambiguity of sentence 7 depends upon the homophony of verbs, it is the case that for each separate lexical item /tərn/ we have homophony of the phonological form of the root, and so naturally for the person–number-tense marker. In sentence 8, however, the morpheme /mawθ/ is unaffected, and the ambiguity rests solely on the homophony of the various lexical items represented by that pronunciation.

Whereas the preceding examples represent one type of ambiguity that results at a surface, phonological level, there are other phonological processes that play a part in riddling. Specifically, word stress and juncture (i.e., pause phenomena) may contribute to the creation of ambiguity in the riddle. Let us consider word stress first. Word stress is utilized in riddling to create ambiguity by playing on the difference between a compound word and a phrase which, although it has the same morphemic content as the compound, is composed of a modifier plus a noun. For instance, consider the difference between the utterances of the phrases *hothouse* (compound) and *hot house* (modifier plus noun), where the former is a place to grow plants and the latter is a very warm domicile. Regardless of spelling conventions, these words are distinguished by the placement of primary stress in their pronunciations. In the compound, primary stress is placed on the first syllable, with a lesser degree (tertiary stress) being placed on the second syllable, giving us a phonological representation /háthàws/ (´ indicates primary stress, ` indicates tertiary stress). In the combination of modifier plus noun, however, the stress pattern is different. In this case primary stress is on the second syllable of the combination, with secondary stress (marked as ^) on the first syllable. It is this difference in stress patterns that in English provides the basis for distinguishing compounds from modifier plus noun constructions, with their differing semantic content.

This difference may be exploited in riddling. Consider, for example, riddles like those in sentences 10, 11, 12, and 13.

10. What bird is lowest in spirits? *Bluebird.*
11. What weapon does an angry lover resemble? *Cross-bow.*
12. When is a black dog not a black dog? *When it is a greyhound.*
13. When did Moses sleep five in a bed? *When he slept with his forefathers.*

In sentence 10 we find an example parallel to the explanatory illustration just presented. The riddle asks for a particular species of bird that is sad. Of course, such a determination is impossible in the real world. However, if a bird were to be sad, such a bird would indeed be a blue bird /blûwbə́rd/. The riddle exploits this possible modifier-plus-noun sequence by ignoring the fact that its stress pattern differs from that of a corresponding compound, /blúwbə̀rd/. This suspension of stress pattern distinctions is facilitated in English by the fact that we may use what is called *contrastive stress* to emphasize any word in an utterance, simply by shifting primary stress to that word. Thus, the riddler, in revealing the answer to sentence 10, can emphasize the adjective *blue*, thus shifting the primary stress to that adjective, whereas it otherwise would fall on the noun being modified. The result is that the new modifier-plus-noun construction, with its contrastive stress, is practically homophonous with the compound word.

In sentences 11–13 we find similar contrasts of compound words with modifier-plus-noun constructions. However, in these cases the constituents of the constructions are homophonous, rather than identical, as was the case in sentence 10. So in sentence 11, although both the weapon /krásbòw/ and the lover /krâsbów/ have a basic adjective-plus-noun source, we have in fact two separate lexical items that correspond to the pronunciation /kras/ and two lexical items that are pronounced /bow/. We see, then, that the ambiguity in sentence 11 is complex. First, it involves lexical ambiguity of the type discussed earlier. Second, it plays upon contrasting stress patterns of the homophonous constructions to confuse the riddlee. Indeed, this confusion is made even more complex by the fact that the answer to such riddles may be either the compound (10, 12, 13) or the adjective-plus-noun construction (11). Solving such riddles, then, involves (1) perceiving a lexical ambiguity, (2) recognizing the role of contrastive stress patterns, (3) determining which combination of lexical items and stress patterns serves as the answer to the riddle.

By way of clarifying these claims, let us now consider in some detail riddle 12. The primary lexical ambiguity in this case lies in the distinction between the adjective *gray* and the first morpheme of the compound *greyhound*, both of which are pronounced /grey/. Thus the distinction that is played upon in this riddle is that between a dog that is gray, /grêyháwnd/, and a certain breed of dog, /gréyhàwnd/. We see here, as in 10, that the obvious answer to 12 is /grêyháwnd/, for indeed such a dog is by definition not black. However, the riddler, in giving the answer, employs contrastive stress, shifting the primary stress from /–hawnd/ to /grey–/, making the answer homophonous with the compound word. This same strategy is employed in 13, where the utterances /fôwrfáðərz/ and /fówrfàðərz/ are manipulated. The riddler's advantage is that only he knows which combination of lexical items and stress is being employed in such riddles.

In making the distinction between compound words and sequences of adjective-plus-noun, it should be noted that there is a difference in pronunciation aside from the stress patterns. Namely, in the adjective-plus-noun combinations, there is a slight pause between the two constituents, whereas no such pause occurs in the pronunciation of compounds. Thus, a more accurate representation of the constructions being manipulated in 10, for example, would be /blúwbə̀rd/ versus /blûw + bə́rd/, where / + / represents the pause phenomenon that we call juncture.

Occasionally there are instances of utterances in English that are distinguished primarily by the presence or absence of juncture. Consider, for example:

14. /náytrèyt/

which, depending upon placement of juncture, may mean either a chemical compound containing NO_3 or the cost of an airplane ticket after 6:00 P.M. The former reading is represented adequately by 14, but the latter possesses a pause (juncture) by which it is to be distinguished from 14, /náyt + rèyt/. Notice that the stress is identical in these two cases, so that the placement of juncture is the distinguishing feature.

We see that juncture is used to distinguish utterances that would otherwise be homophonous, and therefore ambiguous. It is not surprising, then, that juncture is in the riddler's repertoire of ambiguity-creating devices. Consider riddle 15:

15. Why is a man clearing a hedge in a single bound like a man snoring? *He does it in his sleep* (*his leap*).

The ambiguity played upon in this case results from the placement of juncture in the utterance /hIzliyp/. We should first point out that *his sleep* consists technically of two separate lexical items, pronounced in isolation as /hIz/ and /sliyp/. In speech, however, the final /z/ and initial /s/, which are both alveolar fricatives, elide, resulting in the articulation of one sound, /z/, which serves double duty as a final and initial consonant simultaneously. It is this process of elision that produces /hIzliyp/, which is homophonous with *his leap*. This utterance, in turn, is subject to different interpretations, depending upon placement of juncture. Thus, *his sleep* can be represented as /hI + zliyp/, whereas *his leap* can be represented as /hIz + liyp/. We should note here that both phrases consist grammatically of a possessive pronoun and a noun, so that the homophony in this case occurs within a given grammatical construction, the elements of which must be discerned by the riddlee. An interesting note here is that in riddles like 15 the "answer" is the ambiguous utterance, rather than one of the possible utterances that serve as the question. That is, the answer to 15 depends upon the creation of ambiguity rather than on its resolution.

A similar case involving juncture is seen in riddle 16:

16. When is it hard to get your watch out of your pocket?
    When it keeps sticking (*keeps ticking*) *there.*

Here, the utterance *keeps sticking* is pronounced in ordinary speech as /kiypstIkIŋ/, making it homophonous with *keeps ticking*. As with 15 we find an elision of alveolar fricatives, so that in the former phrase, /s/ serves simultaneously as a final and an initial consonant. The only basis for distinguishing the two phrases is by the placement of juncture, so that the former is represented by /kiyp + stIkIŋ/. We see here again that the grammatical forms involved are the same, in this case the verb *keep* plus a present participle. Again as in 15, the wit of this riddle depends upon the ambiguity being present in the answer, not in the question.

This makes an important point concerning the role of ambiguity in the riddle. For we see from examples like 15 and 16 (and 10–13, as well) that it is not the case that the ambiguity involved in a riddle is necessarily contained in the question. Rather, it is the case that the wit of the riddle depends on the resolution of an ambiguity somewhere in the riddle structure, which includes the answer as well as the question. We see, then, that the consideration of wit in the riddle must encompass more than traditional studies have indicated (cf. our discussion of the definition of the riddle, chapter 5). For to understand the wit involved in riddling, it is necessary to scrutinize the entire structure of the riddle act to determine at what point the element of wit (through ambiguity) is introduced.

There is one last category of phonologically-based riddles that must be treated. These riddles are concerned with minimal phonemic pairs, i.e., with words used to contrast the phonemes of English. Thus, to return to an earlier example, we saw that the difference between /pɛt/ and /bɛt/ lies in the distinction between /p/ and /b/, since the pronunciations of these two words are otherwise identical. Such pairs of words, which are distinguished by only one phoneme, are called "minimal pairs." There are riddles that exploit minimal pairs, as in riddles 17 and 18.

17. What is the difference between a baby and a coat? *One you wear, one you were.*
18. What is the difference between a ballet dancer and a duck? *One goes quick on her legs, the other goes quack on her legs.*

In 17 the minimal pair played upon in /wɛr/ versus /wər/, where the minimal distinction is based upon the difference between /ɛ/ and /ə/. In 18 the minimal pair is /kwIk/ and /kwæk/, where /I/ and /æ/ are contrasted.

It is interesting here that the element of wit involved is not ambiguity, but rather another aspect of what Abrahams 1972 has called "word resiliency." In this case the resiliency consists of using minimal pairs as phonological distinctions to make a comparison between two referents that are not apparently comparable. Although such examples do not fall within our categories of ambiguity, they do represent a conscious effort to manipulate the phonological level of grammar to produce wit.

We see, then, that what is traditionally regarded as wit in riddles can be partially related to the creation of ambiguity in the riddle form. In this chapter we have explored how ambiguity can be produced by the manipulation of the phonology of English. In chapter 3 we shall explore the role of ambiguities produced at the morphological and syntactic levels in creating wit. We shall then relate the linguistic aspects of wit to the broader context of riddling.

1. For purposes of simplicity, in underlying structures such as those in figures 3 and 4 we shall omit unnecessary elements such as articles and tense markers throughout this work.

2. In the cases to be discussed, "phonological" refers to lexical ambiguity of phonemic form, stress, and juncture. Thus, our use of the term "phonological" is more precisely characterized than that of Ben-Amos 1976.

GRAMMATICAL STRATEGIES

Chapter Three

IN THIS CHAPTER WE shall explore the exploitation of morphology and syntax in producing wit in riddles. We shall also consider the interaction of phonological, morphological, and syntactic strategies in creating the block elements of riddles. In dealing with morphological ambiguity, we find two types of grammatical manipulation. The first is similar to the morphological ambiguity described in chapter 2; i.e., it is a play on the homophony of two morphologically different constructions. So, for instance, we find riddles like those in sentences 1 and 2.

1. What's black and white and red all over? *Newspaper.*
2. Why is coffee like the soil? *It is ground.*

In sentence 1 we find homophony of a simple lexical item /rɛd/ and a verb plus its past participle morpheme, /rɛd/. This latter form must be interpreted morphologically as /riyd/ + /–d/, where /–d/ is the regular past participle morpheme in English. However, /riyd/ falls into the category of verbs known as irregular, which means that its past tense and past participle markers do not conform to the normal rules for forming these inflectional forms. Thus, /riyd/ may be classed with such verbs as /bliyd/ (past participle /blɛd/) and /liyv/ (past participle /lɛft/), where the past participle forms, as well as the past tense forms, must be learned by rote, rather than by rule.

In sentence 2 we find a similar instance of morphological

ambiguity. Here, the lexical item /grawnd/, a noun, is homophonous with the past participle of the verb /graynd/. We should note here that in cases like 1 and 2, the syntax of the ambiguous utterances differs on the various readings. Thus, the answer to 2, *It is ground*, has two possible underlying structures, depending upon whether /grawnd/ is a noun or a verb form as in figure 9 and figure 10. So in figure 9 we have a simple predicate noun, where the form of the verb *to be* is a copula. In figure 10, however, the situation is quite different. For in order for the surface structure of figure 10 to mirror that of figure 9, several things must happen. First, the sentence must be passivized. This entails moving the indefinite subject NP *someone* to the end of the sentence into a *by*-phrase (i.e., making it *by someone*) and moving the object NP *it* into subject position. At the same time, the verb /graynd/ must be made passive by inserting the verb *to be* with the past participle of /graynd/. These processes yield an intermediate stage of derivation roughly like sentence 3.

3. It is ground by someone.

This structure is homophonous with that of figure 9 except for the phrase *by someone*. In English, as noted above, we may delete unspecified, i.e., indefinite NPs, if this deletion does not destroy the sense of the sentence. In 3, then, we

Figure 9

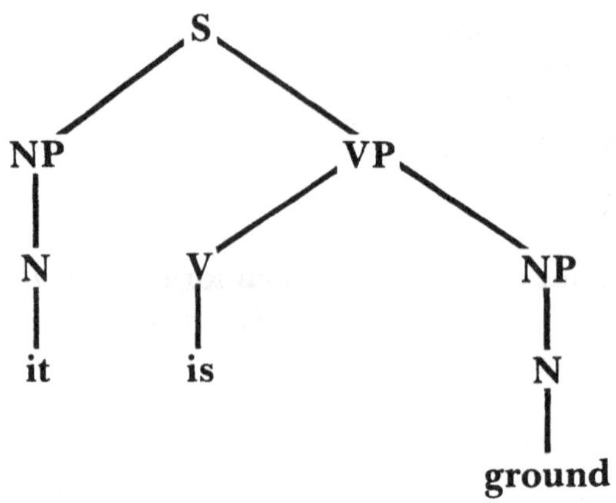

Figure 10

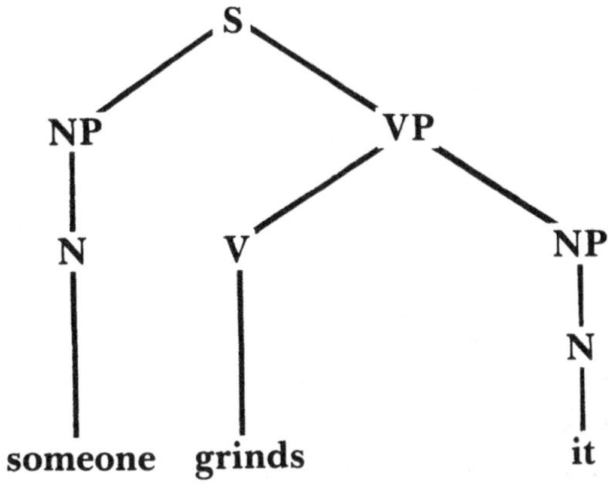

may delete *by someone*, thus yielding the so-called "agentless passive," or "impersonal passive" of English, in this case *It is ground*.

It could be argued, then, that the difference between 1 and 2 is syntactic, rather than morphological. But such an argument misses an important point. Let us assume for a moment that /graynd/ is a regular verb in English. As such, its past participle would be /grayndəd/ (cf. /maynd/–/mayndəd/, /sawnd/-/sawndəd/). In this case if we applied all the same processes outlined for the derivation of figure 10, we would end up with sentence 4.

4. It is grinded.

Obviously, this sentence is not homophonous with the sentence represented by figure 9. Thus, even though the syntax of figures 9 and 10 is different, it is the morphology involved that causes the ambiguity. For though we also depend upon syntactic processes to produce similar sentence patterns from figures 9 and 10, it is the irregular morphology of the verb /graynd/ that is the key to producing the ambiguous element upon which the riddle depends.

The point here is that riddles like 1 and 2 clearly involve more than one grammatical level in their composition.

However, in such cases, it is the morphological manipulation that is primary in the creation of ambiguity. It is for this reason that we classify such riddles as morphologically ambiguous, as opposed to syntactically ambiguous. A similar cross-classification was seen in chapter 2 in dealing with stress- and juncture-related riddles. In these cases the various readings of the ambiguous elements of the riddles frequently differed at the morphological level or the syntactic level. However, the overriding factor in each case was the placement of stress or juncture, so that we classified these riddles by the *primary* source of grammatical ambiguity.

Other riddles that function like 1 and 2 include:

5. When is a rope like a child at school? *When taut* (*taught*).
6. What is the best butter on earth? *A goat*.
7. When is a doctor most annoyed? *When he is out of patients* (*patience*).
8. What musical instrument should one not believe? *A lyre* (*liar*).

In 5 we find that the situation is parallel to that in 1 and 2, where the past participle of /tiyč/ is homophonous with the adjective /tat/. In 6 the ambiguity lies in the word /bətər/, which is either a simple lexical item or a complex form composed of /bət/ plus the agentive suffix /–ər/. In 7 the plural of the noun /peyšənt/ is homophonous with the simple lexical item /peyšənts/. And in 8 we find another situation like 6, in which the simple lexical item /layər/ is homophonous with the complex word /lay/ plus the agentive suffix /–ər/.

We note here that such riddles depend upon oral transmission for their effectiveness. For when they are written, one must frequently explain the relationship of the spelling to the morphology and phonology involved, e.g., that the word *taught* is homophonous with in 5 is *taut*. This may be done in writing by listing both answers, as we have done in several instances.

Another set of strategies for creating morphological ambiguity in riddles involves the arbitrary division of words into their morphemes, and then the use of these morphemes as if they were independent lexical items. So, for instance, consider riddles like those in sentences 9, 10, and 11.

9. What kind of bow can you never tie? *A rainbow.*
10. What kind of ears does a train have? *Engineers.*
11. What room can no one enter? *A mushroom.*

In fact, these examples represent not a single class of morphological strategy for riddling, but three separate classes. The first, exemplified by 9, simply takes the component morphemes of a word and treats them as free lexical items. Thus the *-bow* of *rainbow* is a morpheme that constitutes a part of the larger word. The same strategy is exemplified in riddles like:

12. What driver is never arrested? *A screwdriver.*
13. On what side of a country church is the graveyard? *The outside.*

In these cases again, the morphemes, *-driver* and *-side*, are treated as if they were isolated words, rather than meaningful constituents of larger words.

Examples 10 and 11 may at first appear to use the same type of morphological strategy, but closer examination reveals that they are indeed of different types. In 10 the phonological sequence /iyrz/ (spelled either *ears* or *-eers*) is the block element. Unlike 9, however, the morpheme that is used as if it were an isolated word is not the same morpheme that appears in the resolution, but is merely another, homophonous morpheme. Thus in 9 the morpheme *-bow* is part of the word *rainbow*. In 10 the morpheme *ear* is not the same as the suffix *-eer* that appears in the word *engineer*. Such riddles as 10, then, employ not only the morphological strategy described for 9, but also employ the homophony of different morphemes to confuse the riddlee, i.e., a type of lexical ambiguity.

Other riddles that operate like 10 are:

14. Which miss is most unpopular? *Misfortune.*
15. What ship has two mates but no captain? *Courtship.*

In 14 the independent morpheme meaning a woman is played against the negative prefix, both pronounced /mIs/. In 15 the independent morpheme meaning a sailing vessel is played against a nominalizing suffix, both pronounced /šIp/. In both instances, as in 10, the apparently independent morpheme is homophonous with a morpheme contained in the answer to the riddle, but is not in fact an occurrence of this morpheme.

Although morphological manipulation is the central factor here, the syntax of such riddles also helps to confound the riddlee. For in each case, the riddle question is one that treats the morpheme being used ambiguously as if it were a noun. That is, in each case the riddle question contains an interrogative pronoun *what*, that indicates (misleadingly) to the riddlee that a question is being asked regarding the specification of a particular noun. The riddlee's error is that he assumes that the noun being questioned is the one that appears in the riddle question, when this is not the case.

It should again be noted that these riddles depend upon oral transmission. Thus, for instance, in 10 or 12, where the ambiguous morpheme is spelled differently in its use in the riddle question from the way it appears in the larger morphemic construction of which it is a part in the resolution (*-eer* vs. *ear* and *mis-* vs. *miss*), a written explanation becomes cumbersome and detracts from the riddle.

Yet another morphological strategy is revealed in examples like 11. In this instance a sequence of phonemes that is homophonous with a morpheme, /ruwm/, is treated as if it were an independent morpheme. However, once the answer to the riddle is revealed, it is seen that this sequence of phonemes is not a morpheme of the larger word, i.e., *-room* is not a meaningful constituent of *mushroom*. In other words, the riddle may treat a sequence of phonemes as if it were an occurrence of a given morpheme, when in fact it is not an occurrence of that morpheme, or of any *morpheme*, in order to confuse the riddlee. Other riddles that employ this strategy are:

16. What is the key to a good dinner? *A turkey.*
17. What chins are never shaved? *Urchins.*
18. What pets make the sweetest music? *Trumpets.*

In each of these examples, the riddle question asks for specification of an apparently independent lexical item, *key*, *chins*, and *pets*. However, these apparent lexical items are not morphemes extracted from larger words, or ambiguous morphemes, but merely sequences of phonemes that are homophonous with certain morphemes. Thus, the *-key* of *turkey* has nothing to do with an instrument for unlocking a door, nor with any other definition of the word *key*. Similarly, the *-chins* of *urchins* has nothing to do with the human anatomy, nor does the *-pets* of *trumpets* relate to animals. Such sequences of phonemes that are treated as morphemes may be referred to as *pseudomorphemes*.

This same strategy employing pseudomorphemes can be seen in riddles like:

19. What kind of cat do you find in the library? *Catalogue*
20. What toe never gets a corn? *Mistletoe*
21. What is the gentlest kind of spur? *Whisper*

Here again we see the creation of pseudomorphemes—sequences of phonemes that are homophonous with English morphemes but which themselves are devoid of semantic content. Thus, the /kæt/ of /kætəlag/, the /tow/ of /mIsəltow/ and the /spər/ of /wIspər/ are not semantically related in any way to the actual morphemes they resemble, and so cannot be considered real morphemes. In the riddle act, however, only the riddler knows that the forms in question are pseudomorphemes, and he uses this knowledge to confuse and outwit the riddlee.

As was the case above, such riddles are dependent upon oral transmission, since examples like 21 require an explanation of the interrelationships of spelling, morphology, and phonology.

We turn now to the level of syntax in characterizing the role of ambiguity in riddling. We find that the syntax of English may be manipulated in several ways to create ambiguity in the riddle form. The first way, as outlined in chapter 2, is through *phrase structure ambiguity*, whereby two different underlying syntactic structures have identical surface structures as a result of the homophony of contrasting parts of speech. The second way is through *transformational ambiguity*, where two different underlying structures have identical surface structures by virtue of the transformational processes that apply in the derivations of the surface forms. Two basic types of transformations are used to create ambiguity in riddles: rearrangement and deletion transformations. A *rearrangement transformation* is simply any transformation that rearranges the order of constituents in a phrase structure. So, for instance, passivization is a rearrangement transformation which, given a structure like that in figure 11, moves the NP *Mary* into surface subject position and the NP *John* to the end of the sentence into a *by*-phrase, yielding *Mary was hit by John*. Another common rearrangement transformation is *Question Formation*, which converts a structure like figure 12 into the sentence *Who did John hit?* by moving the indefinite NP *someone* (after it has been changed into an interrogative pronoun) to initial position in the sentence. As we shall see, this transformation is frequently employed in the riddle form.

Deletion transformations are simply those that allow some element to be deleted from a phrase structure tree. One such transformation, Unspecified Pronoun Deletion, is discussed in chapter 2. Thus, there are three basic syntactic processes that may be utilized in creating ambiguity in riddles. Let us now examine each in turn.

Figure 11

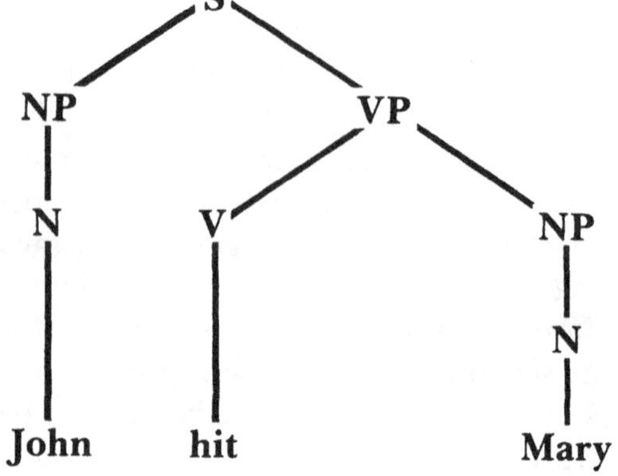

Figure 12

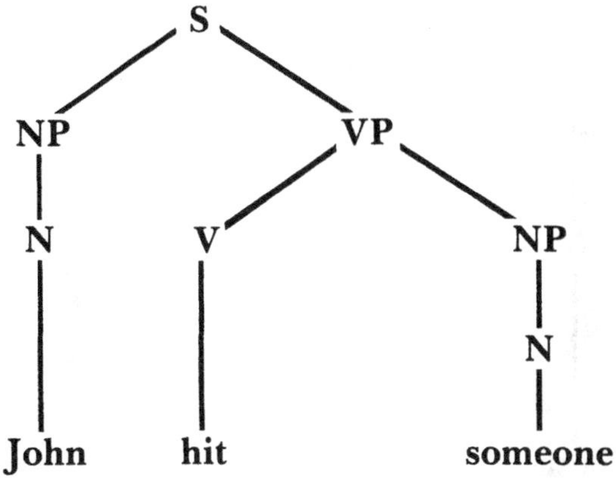

The exploitation of phrase structure ambiguity is comparatively rare in riddling, but can be seen in riddles like:

22. Why is a goose like an icicle? *Both grow down*

23. When is a boy like a pony? *When he is a little horse*

The ambiguity in this case can be seen by examining the underlying syntactic representations involved in the confusing element of the riddle. Thus, the ambiguity in *Both grow down* is resolved in the possible underlying structures in 13 and 14. We see here that in figure 13 *down* is a direct object, and so an NP, but in figure 14 *down* is an adverb.

Example 23 manifests the same type of syntactic strategy. In this case the crucial element is the phrase /lItəl howrs/, which is either an adjective-noun combination or an adverb-adjective combination. This is shown by contrasting the two underlying structures as in figures 15 and 16. At this point we should note the difference between riddles like those under discussion and those we have called lexically ambiguous in preceding chapters. Simply, in lexically ambiguous riddles we find two homophonous words that are the same parts of speech and that are not distinguishable syntactically in the riddle in which they are employed, for example, the word *turns* in "What turns but never moves?

Figure 13

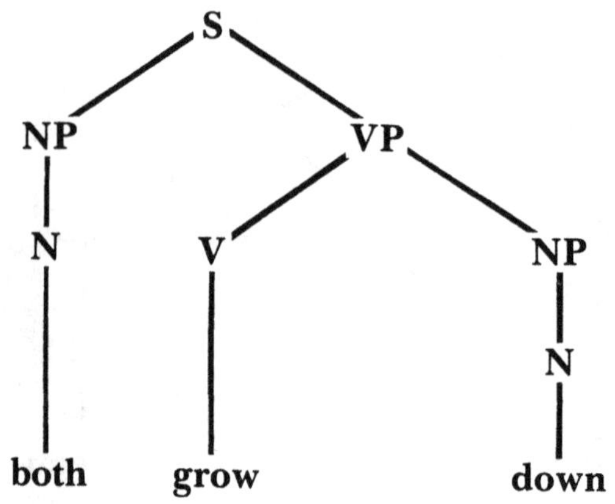

Figure 14

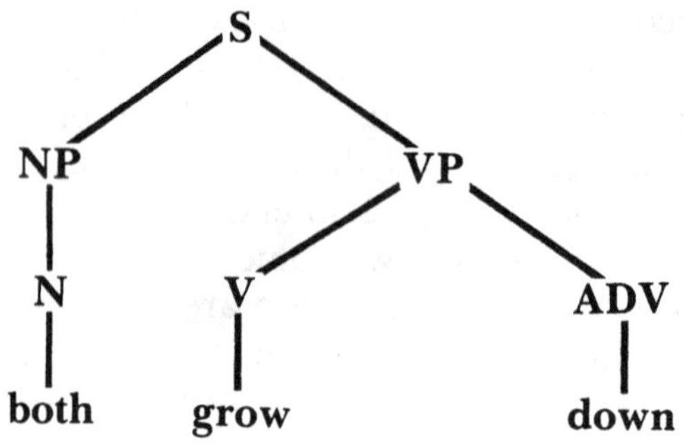

Figure 15

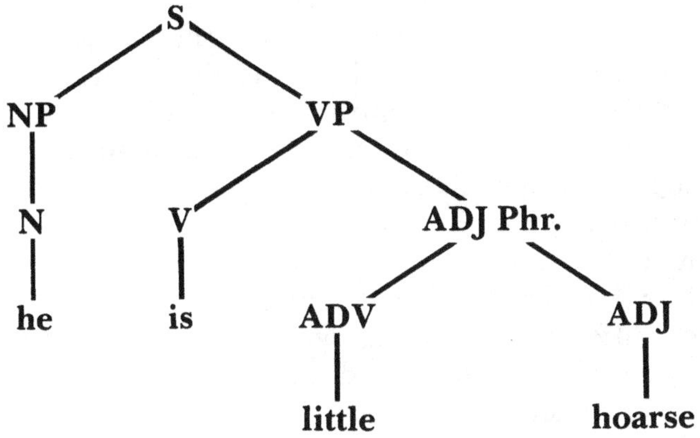

Figure 16

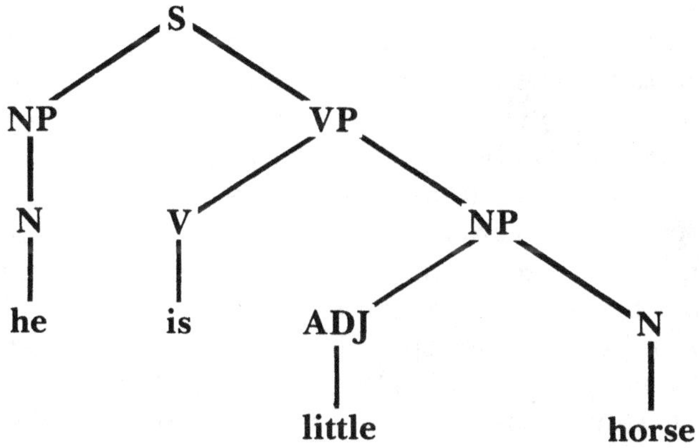

Milk." In the case of phrase structure ambiguity, we have homophony that results when two syntactically different constituents, for example, a noun and an adjective as in example 23, may occur within a string of words in such a way that the syntactic parsing of the sentence is unclear. Thus, in these latter cases, it is the grammar, and not merely the lexicon, that is central to the creation of ambiguity. The fact that the word order does not distinguish the two syntactic structures enables the riddler to use the homophonous constructions as the core of his riddle. The reason for the rarity of this particular type of ambiguity is, we believe, fairly clear. It is simply the case that the number of instances in which different underlying syntactic structures contain homophonous lexical items and have identical word orders are few in English.

Another type of syntactic ambiguity, transformational ambiguity, is frequently employed in the riddle genre. Taking first examples of deletion transformations, consider riddles like:

24. What do you call a man who marries another man? *Minister.*
25. Would you rather have an elephant kill you or a gorilla? *I'd rather the elephant kill the gorilla.*
26. When is a man like a snake? *When he is rattled.*

In each of these cases, ambiguity is created when the deletion of some element from an underlying structure makes this structure homophonous with another, different structure. So, for instance, in 24, we find that the phonological form /mæriy/ may have two semantic representations, which in turn have different syntactic reflexes. One representation designates a formal commitment made between two people and can be represented by the tree in figure 17. The other representation designates a state in which one person performs a ceremony that involves two other people and can be expressed in figure 18. It can be seen from these structures that the configuration of figure 18 is syntactically like that of figure 17, except that figure 18 has an additional prepositional phrase (PP). However, if the NP of the PP in figure 18 is unspecified, it can, as we have seen, be deleted.

Figure 17

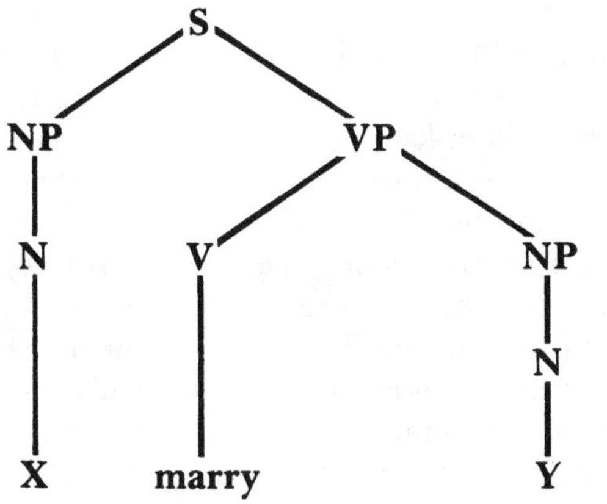

Figure 18

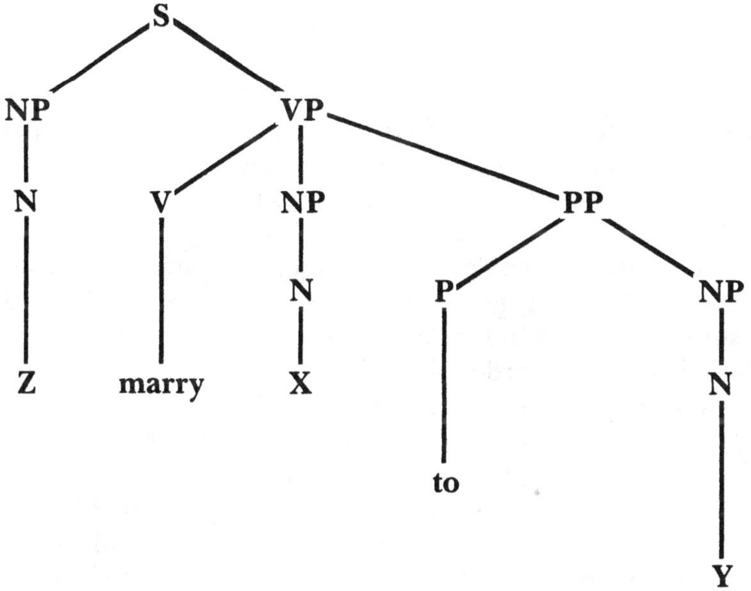

This deletion then leaves the structure in figure 18 syntactically identical to that in figure 17. This being the case, only a larger conversational context can distinguish which semantic representation is intended, since the syntax can no longer serve this function. Naturally, in riddling, there is no larger conversational context upon which to draw. Therefore, only the riddler knows in asking the riddle in 24 that he is employing the semantics represented by the construction in figure 18, and not figure 17. This fact is revealed to the riddlee in the answer, since the NP *minister* represents the third party in the second representation of /mæriy/ described above. The riddlee then realizes that the underlying structure of the question in 20 is really something like "What do you call a man who marries another man to someone?" He understands then that *to someone* has been deleted, as discussed previously.

In 25 we find another case of ambiguity caused by deletion. In this case the two underlying syntactic structures involved are illustrated in figures 19 and 20. In this case we are dealing with the deletion of identical repeated elements in underlying structure. So, in figure 19 we may delete the VP of S_4, since it is identical to that in S_3. We might point out here that this deletion rule is the same one that yields sentences like *John and Mary went to the store* from *John went to the store and Mary went to the store*, where the second *went to the store* (i.e., the VP) is deleted under identity with the first, and the subject NPs are then conjoined.

In figure 20 we can delete the subject *elephant* and verb *kill* of S_4 under identity with the corresponding elements of S_3. Notice that after the deletions in figures 19 and 20, the only element left in S_4 is *gorilla*. However, in figure 19 it is left as a subject NP, and in figure 20 it is left as an object NP, even though the word orders in figures 19 and 20 are identical otherwise after the permissible deletions. Thus, 25 asks either which of two animals you would rather have kill you (figure 19), or whether you would prefer to have an elephant kill you or have the elephant kill a gorilla (figure 20).

In riddle 26 we find another case of Unspecified Pronoun Deletion causing ambiguity. Thus, on one reading the

Figure 19

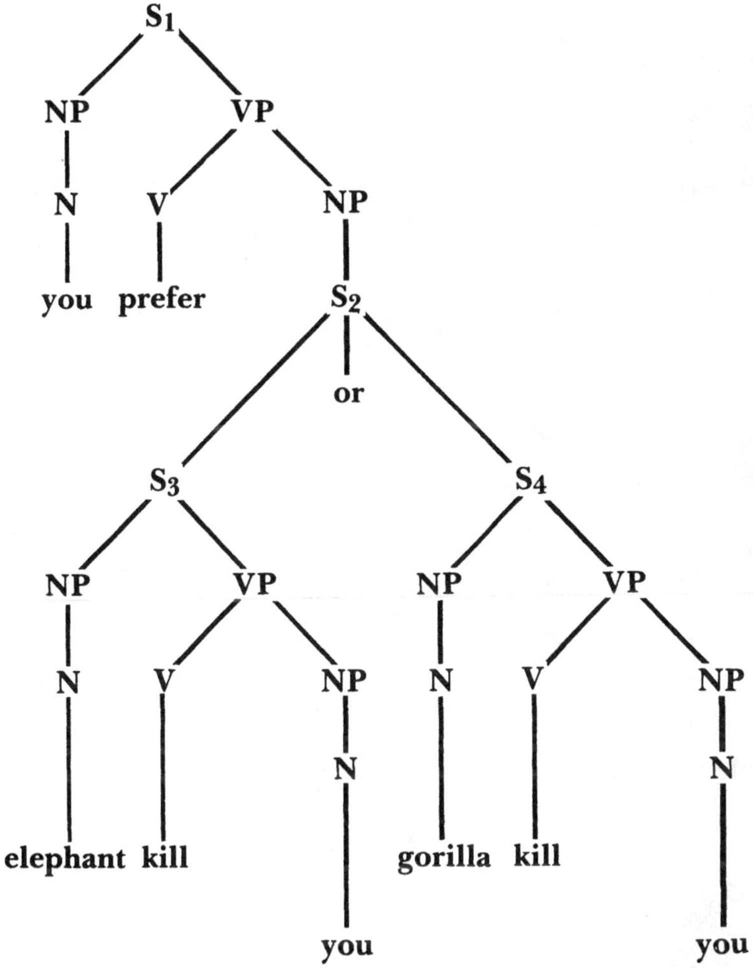
S1
NP
VP
N
V
NP
you
prefer
S2
or
S3
S4
NP
VP
NP
VP
N
V
NP
N
V
NP
N
N
elephant
kill
gorilla
kill
you
you

Figure 20

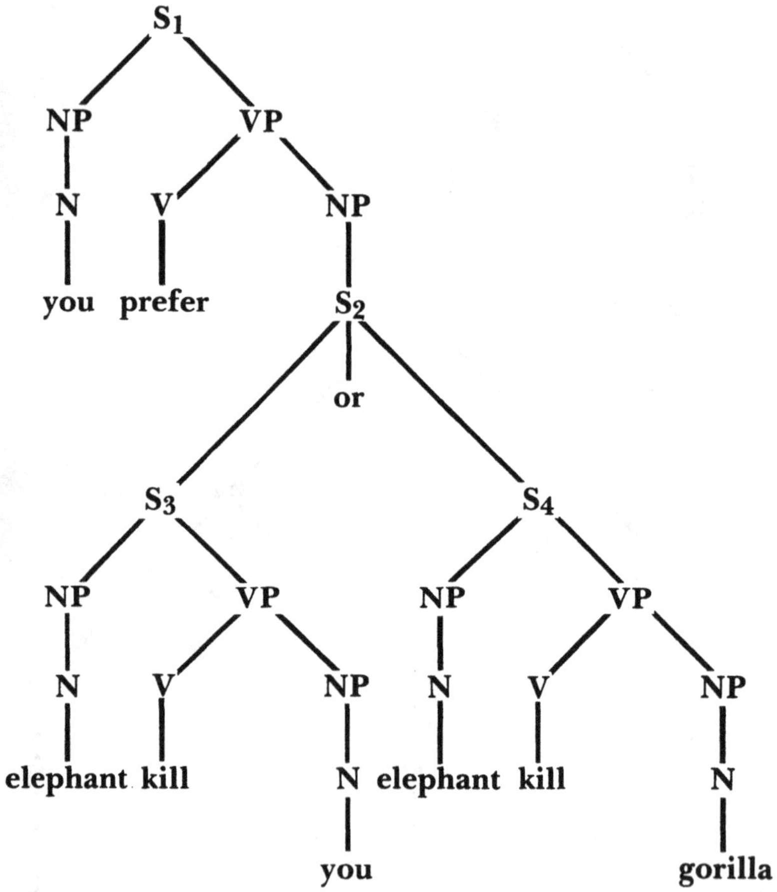
S1
NP
VP
N
V
NP
you
prefer
S2
or
S3
S4
NP
VP
NP
VP
N
V
NP
N
V
NP
elephant
kill
N
elephant
kill
N
you
gorilla

answer to 26 is merely an adjective *rattled*, meaning "having a rattle," and referring to a snake (see figure 21). On the other reading, *rattled* is part of passive construction that can be roughly rendered as "The man is rattled by something," coming from an underlying structure like that in figure 22. As was the case above, the unspecified pronoun and its preposition can be deleted from the passive construction, thus rendering the constructions in figures 21 and 22 homophonous.

We turn now to cases in which a movement transformation causes ambiguity. In such cases it is the Question Formation transformation of English that is utilized. The basic strategy employed is to question some constituent of an idiom, thus pretending that the idiom is a normal syntactic construction. To clarify this statement, let us consider the nature of idioms. They are expressions whose meanings cannot be discerned from the constituent words of the expressions, or from the syntax of the expressions. So, for instance, if we take the idiom "kick the bucket" in *John kicked the bucket*, meaning "John died," we find that we cannot perform any transformations on the idiom and still retain the idiomatic meaning. Thus, a question-and-answer sequence like:

Q: What did John kick?
A: John kicked the bucket.

Figure 21

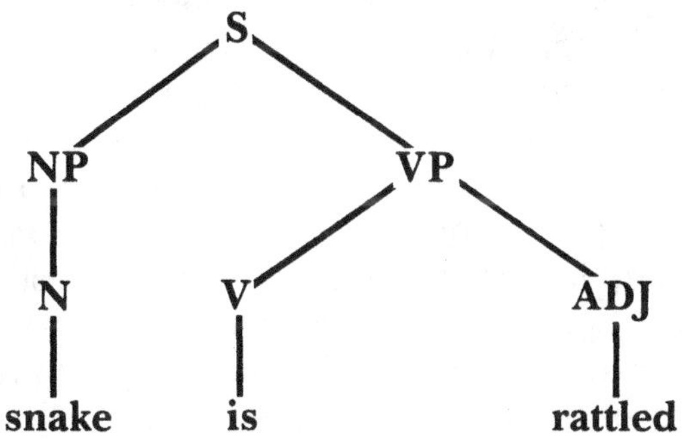

Figure 22

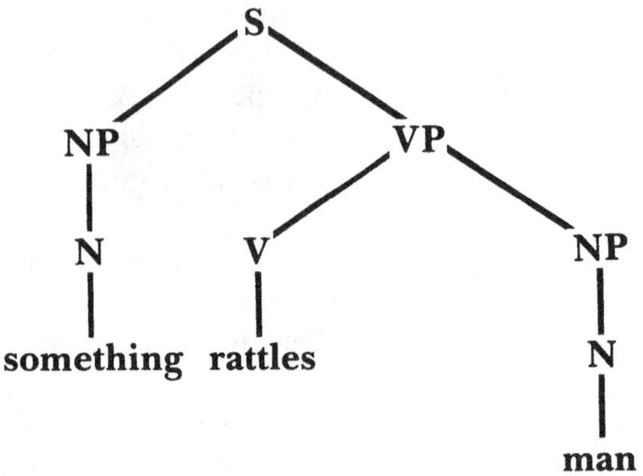

cannot refer to John's death, but only to an event whereby John struck a bucket with his foot.

Similarly, we find that idioms do not undergo various other movement transformations, e.g., passivization. Thus, a sentence like *The bucket was kicked by John* cannot refer to John's death. These examples point to the fact that idioms are frozen syntactic constructions with fixed meanings. That is, since the meaning of an idiom is not derived from its component parts, the only way to recognize an idiom is by its fixed (frozen) syntax. Thus, it is not surprising that idioms do not undergo many transformations, since a change in syntactic pattern renders an idiom indistinguishable from a construction that is composed of the same constituents as the idiom but that does have a meaning derivable from its constituents, i.e., a literal meaning. Therefore, in our example, any syntactic manipulation of the idiom *kick the bucket* meaning "die" makes it indistinguishable from the literal meaning of the ordinary phrase *kick the bucket*.

In riddling, however, we find that the restrictions on transformations of the syntax of idioms may be violated to confuse the riddlee. That is, the riddler is free to question any element of an idiom as if it were not an idiom, but a literal statement. This immediately creates ambiguity, since the riddler is using both the literal and idiomatic meanings of a given syntactic construction to confound the riddlee. Consider, then, riddles like:

27. What is it you will break if you even name it? *Silence.*
28. When is a lamp in bad humor? *When it is put out.*
29. What does a person grow if he works hard in his garden? *Tired.*
30. What goes most against a farmer's grain? *A reaper.*

In 27 the idiom *to break (the) silence* is violated by questioning the NP *silence*. In so doing the riddler is apparently asking a question about an object that is extremely fragile. It is only in revealing the answer that it becomes clear that we are dealing with an idiom and not a literal statement.

In 28 we find a variation on idiom manipulation. Here the ambiguous syntactic construction *put out* is the answer to the riddle, and the effect of the riddle depends upon the recognition of both the idiomatic and literal senses of the construction. Here, as we discussed above, the riddle hinges not so much on the resolution of ambiguity as on its creation.

In 29 Question Formation has been employed to obscure the differences between the literal use of the word *grow* and its figurative sense "become" in the idiom *to grow tired*. Thus, the interrogative pronoun *what* apparently is questioning an NP that would be the direct object of *grow*, thus suggesting a literal interpretation of the verb. When the answer is revealed, however, we see that in fact two syntactic violations have served to confuse the riddlee. First, the interrogative pronoun *what* can be used only to question NPs, and we find that in the idiomatic answer to the riddle, *tired* is in fact an adjective. Second, the idiom *to grow tired* does not allow the application of Question Formation to *tired*, so that no question can be asked of this idiom, the answer to which is *tired*.

In 30 we find a case where the riddle question contains an ambiguity of literal vs. idiomatic interpretation of the expression *go against the grain*. The ambiguous adverb *most* in this instance serves to steer the riddlee toward the idiomatic interpretation, something like "What most annoys a farmer?" In the answer it is revealed that *most* means not "to the greatest extent," but rather "most frequently," and that the question is to be taken literally.

One last category of syntactic processes involved in riddling is that in which a given syntactic construction is homophonous with a morphological construction. The creation of ambiguity in these cases depends upon both morphological and syntactic processes that result in identical phonological (but not morphological or syntactic) forms. Such instances thus represent the interaction of two grammatical levels. Our decision to include these cases under the study of syntactic ambiguity stems from the fact that it is always the case that a series of transformations causes the surface form of an utterance to coincide with another utterance in which regular morphological processes have occurred. In any case, as we have seen, the relationship between morphology and syntax is complex, and these instances of interaction are merely another indication of the closeness of these levels. Consider, then, riddles like:

31. What flowers does a person always carry? *Tulips* (*two lips*).
32. When is a boat like a heap of snow? *When it is adrift.*
33. Why is a fish dealer never generous? *His business makes him selfish* (*sell fish*).
34. Why is a mouse like grass? *The cattle* (*cat'll*) *eat it.*
35. Why can't you starve to death in the desert. *Because of the sandwiches* (*sand which is*) *there.*

In 31 the morphological construction of a noun /tuwlIp/ plus the plural morpheme /–s/ is homophonous with the adjective-noun construction /tuw/ + /lIps/, "two lips." It should be noted here that the homophony, and the resultant ambiguity, of this construction depend on phonological factors, i.e., stress and juncture, as well as on morphological and syntactic processes. Thus the two constructions above could be represented as /túwlÌps/ and /tûw + lÍps/, respectively. However, as discussed above, the use of contrastive stress overrides the normal stress patterns, producing constructions that are completely homophonous.

In 32 we find homophony of an adjective /ədrIft/ and a determiner-noun sequence /ə + drIft/, where in normal conversation no distinction in pronunciation would be made. In fact, in normal conversation the need to distinguish the two would rarely, if ever, arise, since the two constructions are not particularly likely to occur in the same conversational context.

In 33 we contrast an adjective /sɛlfIš/ with a verb-direct object construction /sɛl + fIš/, where stress is again a factor as described above. In 34 we find that the syntactic transformation called Contraction changes the form of /kæt + wIl/, *cat will*, to /kætəl/, *cat'll*, which is homophonous with the noun /kætəl/, *cattle*. And in 35 we find that the head noun of a relative clause, *sand*, along with the relative clause that follows it, *which is there*, is homophonous with the plural of the noun *sandwich* plus the locative *there*.

In all of the riddles 31–35, although ambiguity plays a major role in the wit of the riddles, we cannot help but note that some element of wit must be involved in creating a question that the desired responses must fit. This element of wit clearly is closely allied with the linguistic manipulation with which we are dealing. This last category of riddles serves to especially emphasize the fact that in all riddles a variety of strategies, linguistic or otherwise, are at work simultaneously. The strictly linguistic aspects of wit in riddling that have been discussed represent only one type of cognitive device employed in riddling. This point is driven home in Ben-Amos 1976, which distinguishes "cultural" and "empirical" ambiguity from linguistic ambiguity. Ben-Amos rightly notes that linguistic and cultural aspects of riddling are complementary, rather than mutually exclusive aspects of riddling.

This relationship of language and culture in riddling may be elaborated upon when we consider riddling in comparison to ordinary speech and to cultural performances that are not language-bound. In the first instance, language is a reflection of culture. Since riddling represents a type of artful manipulation, or play, within a culture, we may regard riddling as a type of metacultural play, in that it is an artful manipulation of a basic means of dealing with culture, viz., language.[1] As to the relation of riddling to other types of play in culture, the obvious comparison is with slapstick, physical comedy (see, e.g., Hockett 1977). Slapstick, as riddling, takes events that are considered clumsy or embarrassing in ordinary interactions (e.g., slipping on a banana peel or accidently uttering an ambiguous utterance that hinders communication) and makes them artful in a performance context. This is especially true for the morphological riddles examined, for they involve incomplete or incorrect analyses of word structure in English, i.e., grammatical clumsiness.

This exploitation of maladroitness as an art form is apparent in a type of riddle that plays upon some of the most common types of "slips of the tongue" that plague us all. Specifically, the wit in this type of riddle derives from the reversal of sounds (called *metathesis*) and the reversal of words in a sentence. Such metathesis/reversal phenomena occur in everyday speech, for example, when one says "irrevelant" for "irrelevant," which involves simple metathesis within a word, or when one says "Let me sew you to your sheet" for "Let me show you to your seat," which involves a long-distance metathesis commonly known as a spoonerism. In other cases whole words may be reversed within a sentence, as when one says "I'll mark the hit" for "I'll hit the mark." Let us see, then, how this linguistic clumsiness is utilized in riddling.

A number of riddles employ metathesis, as:

36. What is the difference between a deer fleeing from hunters and a midget witch? *One is a hunted stag, the other a stunted hag.*
37. What is the difference between a fisherman and a dunce? *One baits hooks, the other hates books.*
38. What is the difference between a mouse and young lady? *One harms cheese, the other charms he's.*

In each case the wit of the riddle depends crucially on reversal of initial sounds of words. In other instances it is the reversal of words that makes riddles witty, as in:

39. What is the difference between a jeweler and a jailer? *One sells watches, the other watches cells.*

40. What is the difference between a professional musician and one who hears him? *One plays for his pay, the other pays for his play.*

41. What is the difference between a donkey and a postage stamp? *One you lick with a stick, the other you stick with a lick.*

In such cases we find reversals involving primarily verbs and direct objects or objects of prepositions (i.e., nouns). In each of these examples, we find a verb (*sell*, *play*, *lick*) that becomes an object, whereas an object (*watches*, *pay*, *stick*) becomes a verb in the reversed construction. This reversal depends upon certain verbs and nouns being homophonous, but not necessarily semantically related. This is most apparent in 39, with the homophones *sell* and *cell*.

A related strategy is one whereby the reversal, which involves verbs and objects, exhibits no particular patterning of grammatical elements in the reversal, as in 39–41. Thus we find riddles like:

42. What is the difference between a sewing machine and a kiss? *One sews seams nice, the other seems so nice.*

43. What is the difference between a hungry man and a glutton? *One longs to eat, the other eats too long.*

In 42 the verb-plus-adverb construction *seems so* is contrasted with the verb-plus-direct object *sews seams*, whereas in 43 the infinitive *to eat* is contrasted with the verb-plus-adverb combination *eats too*. Although the neat patterning of verbs and objects seen in 39–41 is not present in these riddles, we do find again that the reversal depends upon homophony between words that are different parts of speech. It is the fact that the homophony is between different grammatical categories that differentiates the strategy of 39–43 from the strategy of simple lexical ambiguity.

The strategies that have been outlined in this chapter, as well as those discussed in chapter 2, permit a rehearsal and reinforcement of grammatical norms through inversion and intensification (see in this regard Abrahams 1973). As has been demonstrated, the riddles treated in this work are drawn from a wide range of linguistic phenomena that are considered accidents in ordinary speech. In riddling we classify our linguistic clumsiness and present it in a way that permits us to control it in a performance context. Thus the riddle genre permits us to demonstrate our lack of command of language, as well our command of language.

1. This notion is more fully treated in many places: Ben-Amos 1971, Abrahams (ms.), Bauman 1975, Hymes 1970, and Burke 1968.

WRITTEN AND VISUAL STRATEGIES

Chapter Four

MANY OF THE RIDDLES we have examined thus far are dependent upon oral transmission for their effect. Riddles like 1 and 2, for example, lose much of their witty element when written, in that concessions to spelling conventions must be made in order to reveal the answers.

1. What's black and white and red (read) all over? *A newspaper.*
2. What kind of ears does a train have? *Engineers.*

There also exists, however, a realm of folk traditions that depends, at least in part, on the written word, for example epitaphs, autograph book rhymes, and graffiti. Although such forms may be transmitted orally, they frequently depend upon a type of visual stimulus or the recognition of a cognitive fit between language and a specific real-world context that goes beyond mere utterance. Many of the principles in this type of folk tradition are realized in riddles, and the specific strategies involve the exploitation of various formal aspects of the roman alphabet and the roman and arabic numeral systems, such as the shapes of the constituent elements of the systems and the names of the elements.

In dealing with riddles that employ such strategies, we shall define the endpoints on a continuum of riddle strategies. At one endpoint are riddles like those discussed in chapters 2 and 3, which depend upon oral transmission; at the other end are riddles that, as we shall show, depend primarily on orthography or visual stimuli to be effective. In the latter category, we count a variety of types that, although transmitted orally, require visual confirmation of the fit between the question and answer, or at least a mental (i.e., a covert, or internalized) recognition of this fit. In the types to be examined, recognition of this fit depends upon a knowledge of English spelling and orthography; the structure of our orthographic system and our spelling conventions are exploited in the formulation of such riddles.

Consider, for example, a riddle like:

3. What makes a road broad? *The letter B.*

This riddle is impossible to render without recourse to orthography. Moreover, such a riddle exploits the fact that words, in addition to being semantic units, are bundles of letters, the referents of which can be changed by the insertion, deletion, or rearrangement of the components of these bundles, e.g., the addition of a *b* to *road* to produce *broad.*

Riddles of this type should be of interest to us because they clearly demonstrate that literacy, rather than leading to the atrophy of traditional forms, may provide the folk with additional devices for verbal play. We shall return to this point in more detail later in this chapter. For now, let us relate the verbal play found in sight and spelling riddles to the type of play found in traditional riddles that exploit linguistic structures at the oral level.

With the introduction of orthographic representations of language, we may observe the addition of another level of confusion to those already employed in the act of riddling. We shall now examine how considerations of spelling and orthography can add another dimension to traditional verbal enigmas. We shall define three types of such riddles: (1) those that exploit the names of letters of the alphabet, (2) those that exploit the relationship between letters of the alphabet and the speech sounds they represent, and (3) those that exploit the shapes of letters and numerals.

The first category listed plays on the fact that the letters of our alphabet (called *graphemes*) have names, as well as phonetic values (i.e., pronunciations). Most letters of our alphabet, in fact, may stand for more than one sound, e.g., the letter *c* may be pronounced /s/, as in *cite*, or /k/, as in *cat*. Each letter has a unique name, however, by which we may unambiguously refer to that letter independently of any phonetic value (e.g., the letter *c* is called /siy/). A number of riddles exploit the fact that names of certain letters, when pronounced in sequence, are homophonous with actual English words, although the sequence of letter names does not itself constitute a word. Thus, we find riddles like:

4. What do the letters x, p, d, n, and c spell? *Expediency.*
5. Spell enemy in three letters. *NME.*

In these cases the sequences of letter names are homophonous with English lexical items. Confusion, the block element, is caused by the fact that, according to orthodox English spelling convention, the sequences of letters in 4 and 5 are semantically empty.

The riddler's strategy here is apparently to induce the riddlee to spell (i.e., to construct according to standard spelling convention) the word in question. Spelling, however, is primarily a visual operation and, thus, a miscue. The proper strategy in this case is to list the names of letters, rather than to spell, for the riddler in these examples is not dealing with the visual-orthographic fit of letters to words, but with the names of letters vis à vis homophonous, but orthographically correct lexical items. Example 4 is a straightforward example of this device.

Example 5 adds another source of confusion for the riddlee. It asks for a combination of three letters having *enemy* as a semantic referent. In this case an answer that conforms both to the constraints of the riddle and to English spelling convention is possible: the word *foe*. The riddler, due to the inherent traditional authority of his role, may reject this synonym for *enemy* as incorrect if he can provide an apt alternative. According to his as yet undisclosed rule for the solution to this riddle, he can provide an even more apt solution. He requires, as with the previous example, letters assembled according to their names, rather than to the dictates of standard spelling. The synonym *foe*, then, by his rules, is incorrect because the sequential listing of letter names *NME* /ɛn + ɛm + iy/ is demanded. This, of course, is impossible to produce without treating the letters as orthographic units with individual names, rather than as orthographic units representing certain phonemes that are combined to form written words. Like 4, then, this example operates by posing a question about language at the visual, written level, and by creating answers by exploiting the phonological values of letters vis à vis the names we give to these orthographic symbols.

A riddling strategy closely related to that just described is seen in riddles like:

6. What are the most sensible letters? *Y's* (*wise*).
7. What letters are most provoking? *T's* (*tease*).
8. How many P's (peas) are in a pint? *One.*

In these cases the plurals of names of letters are exploited for their homophony with actual words. This type of riddle, as the type represented in 4 and 5, depends upon oral transmission for the same reasons as examples 1 and 2. However, unlike 1 and 2, these riddles depend upon more than simple lexical or morphological ambiguity.[1] In these cases the wit of the riddles depends in part on reference to a nonverbal, visual representation of speech. Thus, although such riddles do not require direct visual confirmation of the fit between the questions and answers, they do rely on reference to a visual medium and so are more visually oriented than riddles like 1 and 2.

The second strategy listed above plays upon the conventional orthographic representations of words in English. In such cases the riddler asks for a clarification or specification concerning a word, or the relationship between two words. The answer in such cases turns out to be a letter of the alphabet, thus revealing that the riddle question concerns orthography, i.e., a metasystem, rather than the real world, as the riddlee is led to believe. Thus we find riddles like:

9. What is the end of everything? *G*
10. What changes a lad into a lady? *Y*
11. What changes a pear into a pearl? *L*

These riddles exploit the fact that whereas words are semantic entities (i.e., they are things that refer to concepts, objects, etc.) on the orthographic level, they are also things with a discrete existence (i.e., they are assemblages of letters that have a distinct material reality apart from the concepts to which they refer). This double nature is manipulated to create ambiguity in riddle questions, and, thus, to create a block to solution by the riddlee.

In example 9 the block element results from the fact that we are dealing with two separate lexical items that have identical phonological forms, *everything* /εvriyθIŋ/. On the one hand, this word refers to a concept; on the other it is an orthographic construction. Thus we have an example of simple lexical ambiguity manifested in enigmas that do not play with orthography, such as:

12. What has an eye that never closes? *A needle.*

13. What has a mouth but does not eat? *A river.*

The ambiguous lexical items in 12 and 13 (*eye* and *mouth*), like that in 9 (*everything*), have identical phonological forms, are the same parts of speech, and differ only by semantic features. However, riddle 9 differs from 12 and 13 in critical ways.

Examples 12 and 13 operate strictly on the oral level. The ambiguity results from the phonological identity of various lexical items. They operate on the level of utterance, since with the oral riddle words are ephemeral entities without a separate material existence. With the introduction of another level of complexity, viz., written representation, an additional device for confusion emerges. Example 9 simply does not work without reference to orthography. The aptness of the answer must be visually recognized (either overtly or covertly). The wit of the riddle is not based, then, on the recognition of homophony, but on the treatment of words as bundles of graphemes, discrete and separable from the semantic representations of lexical items. It is only with the introduction of writing as a strategy that such riddles can come into existence.

Examples 10 and 11 also deal with words as bundles of letters. They do not pose questions in the same direct fashion, however. These riddles exploit syntax in order to confuse the riddlee. This, of course, is not permissible in ordinary, utilitarian speech, where distortions of syntax are considered mistakes. In circumscribed enactments, however, such play with grammatical rules is not only permitted, but encouraged. Let us see now how the riddler uses syntax, in addition to spelling exploitations, to outwit the riddlee.

Example 10 is, strictly speaking, a grammatical utterance, but it is misleading. The riddler is actually asking, "What changes (the word) *lad* into (the word) *lady*?" Confusion is created by the use of the indefinite article *a*. Because of this use of *a*, the riddlee's attention is directed to the class of things referred to by the terms *lad* and *lady*. That is, he seems to require information about the orthographic representation of the words. Example 11 involves a similar strategy, again with the use of the indefinite article, so that the syntax of the riddle question misleads the riddlee in his search for a referent.

In normal speech the two conceptual structures in each of 10 and 11, i.e., the ones referring to semantic entities and the ones referring to orthographic forms, would be rendered differently at the surface level. Usually, the omission of the indefinite article in the realization of the latter conceptual structures would suffice to distinguish the two. In cases like 10 and 11, then, the block element results not from the orthodox application of normal syntactic rules as described earlier for oral riddles, but from the riddler's power to willfully manipulate language.

Another strategy closely related to that just described is seen in riddles like:

14. What occurs twice in a moment, once in a minute, but never in a thousand years? *M*.
15. What part of London is in France? *N*.
16. What is always in fashion, yet always out of date? *F*.

Here the information sought from the riddlee is apparently to be derived from the real world, but is in fact based on spelling conventions, i.e., these riddles are questions about the written code itself, rather than about the message it carries.

These last two strategies discussed are more visually oriented than those involving letter names discussed earlier.

Note, for instance, that these riddles, although they are usually delivered orally, work just as well in a written medium. When written, the effective wit of the riddle is reinforced in that the visual fit of the answer to the question is overtly present in the riddle itself. That is, such riddles, when they are written, always contain their own answers.

At this point we must discuss another strategy that contrasts spelling conventions with pronunciation in English. In these cases, however, the exploitation involves sequences of letters, rather than single letters, as in 9–11 and 14–16. Consider, for example, riddles like:

17. What tune does everyone know? *Fortune.*
18. What ants are the largest? *Giants.*
19. What age is served at breakfast? *Sausage.*

At first such riddles appear to be members of the category that includes riddles like 20 and 21, which employ pseudomorphemes to confuse the riddlee.

20. What is the key to a good dinner? *Turkey.*
21. What chins are never shaved? *Urchins.*

However, a close look at 17–19 reveals that these riddles operate differently from 20 and 21. Although 17–19 do indeed play upon what appear to be pseudomorphemes (*tune*, *ants*, *age*), the strategy in these riddles also contrasts spelling with pronunciation. Thus the orthographic sequence *tune* is pronounced /tuwn/ in the riddle question in 17, but is pronounced /čən/ in the answer, *fortune* /fowrčən/. It is thus the sequence of written letters that is central to the wit of the riddle. The same is true of the orthographic sequences *ants* and *age* in 18 and 19, respectively. Thus we have *age* /eyǰ/ contrasted with /əǰ/ in *sausage* /sasəǰ/, and *ants* /ænts/ contrasted with /ənts/ in giants /ǰayənts/.

This last type of riddle is much more visually oriented than any of the previously discussed types, and in fact may be considered to be completely dependent upon a visual solution. That is, the riddle depends crucially on the covert recognition of the fit of graphemes to phonemes, or on an overt recognition of this fit, the latter situation occurring when the riddle is presented in a visual medium, i.e., in writing. This type is thus at the opposite end of the continuum described above from the orally-oriented riddles seen in 1 and 2. We can see here a transition from riddles that are oral in nature, to those that function either in oral or visual form, to those that are exclusively visual in nature.

Let us turn now to the final strategy listed above, that which exploits the shapes of letters and numerals. Here we find three subcategories, the first of which is exemplified by riddles like:

22. What state is round on both ends and high in the middle? *Ohio.*

This riddle exploits both the shape of the letter *o* and the homophony of the orthographic sequence *-hi-* with the adjective *high*. The confusion in this example is created by the fact that the riddlee is led to the supposition that this is a description of the state's physical characteristics. In this case, *-hi-* is a pseudomorpheme.

A related strategy plays on the homography of roman numerals with English letters. Thus we find riddles like:

23. What plant stands for the number four? *IV* (*ivy*).

Actually, this riddle employs a double strategy. First, it plays upon equivalencies between roman and arabic numerals (four = 4 = IV). It then plays upon the fact that the roman numeral is conventionally written in English with the letters we call *i* /ay/ and *v* /viy/, which when pronounced in sequence are homophonous with the noun *ivy* /ayviy/.

A similar example is seen in:

24. What must you add to nine to make it six? *S* (*IX*).

Here we find that the strategy involves not only a correspondence of a roman numeral to a pair of English graphemes, but also the pronunciation not of the *names* of the graphemes, but rather of the conventional *phonetic values* of the graphemes. Another case of this strategy is seen in:

25. Add ten to nothing and what animal does it make? *OX.*

Here we find yet another subtle twist. First, the riddle uses a combination of arabic and roman numerals. It then exploits the fact that this particular combination of numerals is homographous with the English word *ox*, since the arabic zero and the letter *o* correspond, as do the roman ten and the letter *x*. Finally, the riddle exploits the phonetic pronunciation of this combination of graphemes. Riddles 22–25 are quite clearly visual in nature, since the fit of the answer to the question must either be envisioned by the riddlee (covertly) or shown to the riddlee in an overt, written form.

A final type of exploitation of shape is seen in riddles like:

26. Why is the number nine like a peacock? *Remove its tail and it is nothing.*
27. What increases its value by half when turned upside down? *6.*

Example 26, beyond the simile it creates to compare the number nine to a peacock, exploits the homography between part of this number's shape and the arabic numeral *0*. It thus operates on the visual level much as the pseudomorphemic riddles discussed above act on the grammatical level. That is, example 26 treats the numeral 9 as if it is composed of two constituents: one a tail and the other a circle, the latter of which is homographous with an arabic zero. This, of course, is not a legitimate analysis of 9, and so must be treated as a "pseudoanalysis."

Example 27 merely plays on the fact that a 9 turned upside down becomes homographous with the numeral 6. The confusion in this case results from the fact that the riddler appears to be asking about some object in the real world, when in fact he is asking about a formal aspect (viz., the shape) of constituents of the arabic numeral system.

This strategy is rare, since homography of arabic numerals, or of numerals and graphemes, is rare. The same is not true of homophony between numerals and English words (e.g., *one-won*; *two-too*; *eight-ate*); however, we have encountered few riddles that exploit such homophony. Riddles that exploit shape fall at the visual end of the continuum of riddles that we have delineated.

In earlier chapters we saw that oral riddles exploit each linguistically relevant level of language (viz., phonology, morphology, and syntax). We have now seen that similar types of exploitations exist involving various aspects of orthography. These exploitations involve not only the conventional phonological values of graphemes, but also formal or metatheoretical aspects such as the names of the graphemes and their shapes. In this way riddles exploit language visually by artfully manipulating the written medium, just as they manipulate formal aspects of spoken language to create wit. We have seen further that some of this manipulation of written language interacts with oral strategies of riddling, whereas other forms of orthographic play are more properly visual in their focus.

Neither the varieties of spelling and sight riddles, nor the parallelism between manipulation of language at the oral and written levels is surprising when taken in light of the notions of word resiliency and intensification through inversion found in Abrahams 1972 and 1973. In the first instance, word resiliency is as properly applied to written, visual language as to spoken language, so that it is not any more surprising to find that orthography is playfully manipulated than it is to find spoken language used in playful performance. Further, the type of confusion generated by inversion in the riddle forms we have analyzed serves to reinforce orthographic norms by allowing us to rehearse not only our command of the orthographic system, but by allowing us to demonstrate in a performance context various ways in which we are incompetent in our command of the system.

Throughout our discussion we have used the term *visual* to mean both a mental, covert recognition and a material, overt demonstration of the fit of answer to question in the riddle. The riddles we have analyzed all involve the former and may be reinforced by the latter, as has been mentioned. Let us consider for a moment, in an admittedly preliminary manner, the relationship between sight and spelling riddles and other forms that incorporate graphic representations into their performance strategies.

Obviously, on the level of enactment the oral performance of sight and spelling riddles makes them quite different from those genres that are realized only in writing, such as graffiti, autograph book rhymes, and the like. That is, whereas the former play on the literacy of the folk group, they are intended to be uttered as speech, unlike the latter, which exist only as written communication. The following example, a traditional autograph book rhyme, is of interest since it explicitly indicates the relationship between such forms and writing:

> Some write for pleasure,
> Some write for fame,
> But I write simply,
> To sign my name.

Although the riddles that we have discussed do rely on the ability to read and write, it is important to note that, unlike the written forms just mentioned, they are not required to be rendered in tangible visual form. The sight on which the wit of such riddles depends is a type of envisionment, an imagination of their orthographic forms. They are thus dependent upon, yet independent from, written language.

Further, this class of riddles differs from other forms that actually employ drawings or the written word, such as "droodles" or "over and under sentences." The two following examples represent the class of traditional puzzles that are bound to actual graphic representation.

28. once
    4 P.M. = once upon a time
29. r/e/a/d/i/n/g = reading between the lines

Sight and spelling riddles differ from these forms in another critical way. The former rely on a solution that is in one way or another visual. This is especially apparent in our third type of riddle, although it is a strategy in the other two classes, as well. On the other hand, examples 28 and 29 and other puzzles involving drawings or positional clues present visual clues that require an oral translation. This clearly reverses the situation involved in sight and spelling riddles.

The existence of sight and spelling riddles should be of interest to the folklorist for another reason. For most of the history of the discipline, folklorists have considered their domain to be verbal art, the oral forms of expression in society. Although it is true that few would exclude grafitti, epitaph verse, or other written forms from study, these genres have frequently been dismissed as exceptions to the general rule that folk expression is primarily oral and exists apart from literacy. Perhaps few would go so far as Coffin and Cohen 1974, who define the "folk" as those who "express themselves artistically without recourse to reading and writing" (1974:xxvii). Nevertheless, there is yet to come an exact determination of the relationship between literacy and traditional expression among the folk. The examination of sight and spelling riddles should serve to illustrate that what really exists is not two separate avenues of expression, the oral and the written, but a continuum (in the present instance, at least) between those forms that play with language strictly on the oral level and those that incorporate the knowledge of orthography acquired by literacy into the service of wit.

1. Technically, examples 4 and 5 involve lexical ambiguity, since the names of letters are nouns, and correspond when spoken in sequence with actual English nouns; examples 6–8 involve morphological ambiguity in that it is the addition of the plural morpheme to the names of letters that makes these names homophonous with actual English words (which are not plurals).

PERSPECTIVES ON FORM

Chapter Five

WE HAVE NOW DISCUSSED a number of specific strategies used to create wit in the riddle genre. At this point we need to take what has been said in a broader perspective, namely that of the literature that has served to define the role of the riddle, and the riddle form itself, in oral tradition. An examination of the current status of riddle studies, placed in historical perspective, will enable us to define more precisely the value of our analysis for helping to define the folk riddle, both linguistically and culturally.

Let us first characterize briefly the present state of riddle analysis in terms of the structural and cognitive studies that have provided the framework within which the riddle has been defined. Perhaps the earliest structural analysis in terms of basic units is that of Petsch 1899. He sees five basic elements in the riddle form: an introductory frame, a denominative kernel, a descriptive kernel, a block or distractor element, and a concluding frame. Bascom 1949 expands this framework in attempting to define the actual syntactic patterns of riddles, as well as to explain variations on basic patterns of riddling, both in grammar and culture. Somewhat later, Georges and Dundes 1963 seek to define the riddle by internal morphological characteristics. Their unit of structure is the "descriptive element," a pair of which may be in opposition in a riddle, with the referent of the elements to be guessed by the riddlee. Scott 1969 points out that although Georges and Dundes delineate the types of opposition involved in the relationship between descriptive elements, the descriptive element, as a structural unit, remains undefined by them.

Scott himself makes two attempts at classifying riddle structure. In his earlier work (Scott 1965), he seeks to isolate, define, and classify stylistic devices in the riddle from a linguistic base, resulting in a formulaic generalization that characterizes the riddle as a "unit of discourse consisting of an obligatory proposition slot filled by an utterance *p* and an obligatory answer slot filled by an utterance *a*" (1965:69). In Scott 1969 we find a treatment of riddle structure in terms of immediate constituent and topic-comment analyses, to which we shall return in our treatment of linguistic aspects of riddle analysis.

Abrahams 1968 and Abrahams and Dundes 1972 focus on both structural and cognitive aspects of the riddle. On the one hand, these works pay special attention to the Gestalt created by the quality of the fit between riddle description and referent. The discussion of the four means of scrambling the Gestalt in riddles in these works provides a useful classification. On the other hand, Abrahams 1968 turns to more strictly cognitive problems while advancing arguments concerning the rhetorical capacities of riddles to channel antisocial motives into creative and ultimately useful avenues of expression. Applying the argument of Burke 1941 that symbolic action embodies and proposes strategies for confronting problematic situations, Abrahams analyzes the meaning of the act of riddling and the content of representative riddles performed at West Indian wakes.

Abrahams 1972 considers the social meaning of riddling in his attempts to delineate the complex relationship between riddle texts, manner of riddling performance, and social context. It is asserted that a careful analysis should enable the investigator of a culture to discern the folk world view of the group in question. Four important points are stressed in this study: (1) the act of riddling carries the burden of meaning, (2) the riddle's pattern of tension and relief is overtly intended to confuse, (3) riddle constructs play upon word resiliency, and (4) riddling allows for the rehearsal of the group's principles of order.

Another focal point of those cognitive studies that seek to define the nature of the riddle has been the problem of ambiguity in the riddle. Basic in this regard is Hamnett 1967, in which it is claimed that "riddles and riddling may illuminate some of the principles that underlie classification in social action and cognition generally and can, in particular, indicate the role that ambiguities play in the classificatory process" (1967:379). He rightly points out that in riddling, an ambiguous word or element (the block) can be seen as belonging to two or more frames of reference, according to the interpretation forced upon it, and may even be seen as belonging to several frames of reference at once. In this way, says Hamnett, this element mediates between these frames of reference that may otherwise be disparate in nature. Similar, though less precise, statements of the problem of ambiguity in riddles are to be found in Scott 1965, Harries 1971, and Haring 1974. These works all deal with ambiguity as a "semantic fit" that is impaired in the riddle form. The nature of this semantic fit eludes all attempts at characterization, however. More recently, Ben-Amos 1976 deals briefly with the notions of "cultural ambiguity" and "empirical ambiguity," but in a classificatory, rather than an explanatory manner.

Having briefly surveyed a representative sample of relevant literature pertaining to the structure of the riddle and how this structure interacts with the cognitive processes, let us see where this work has led us. If the special issue of the *Journal of American Folklore* under the editorship of Elli Köngäs Maranda (Maranda 1976) may be taken as representative of the emphases of contemporary students of the genre, classificatory and methodological concerns still predominate. We find that the authors of the essays in this collection have generally attempted to apply analytical schemata and methods that have yielded results in other contexts. Thomas A. Burns (Burns 1976), for example, proposes an etic classification for the units of riddling with a methodology derived from sociolinguistics, specifically from the work of Hymes 1970.

The basic concerns of this collection are manifested not only in the fact that most of the studies contained therein are structural, such as the argument in Evans 1976 for a complex thematic structure for entire riddle sessions similar to the syntagmatic patterns described by Propp for the Russian folktale; we find also anthropologically-based studies such as Glazier and Glazier 1976 and Lieber 1976, which advocate the use of riddles as keys to unlock the riddling culture's means of organizing its perceptions. Riddling may, indeed, be a kind of epistemological dialectic, and, of course, the goal of all studies of symbolic action must be the discovery of those basic patterns that are recapitulated in many spheres of activity. Before moving to such ends, however, we would argue that means must be understood as fully as possible. This, we believe, has not been done, for one often gets the impression that riddles and riddling have now become peripheral to the phenomenological concerns of many contemporary riddle scholars.

In order to reach any conclusions on the ways in which riddles function as perceptual devices, we are obliged to subject these constructions to proper analysis as language. Beginnings have been made, but for the most part these deal only with riddles from a purely literary perspective or make use of the terminology rather than the methodology of linguistics. We shall discuss these presently. In the light of the works just outlined, a new orientation seems to be imperative if for no other reason than the fact that a significant number of these essays continue to belabor "old business," ranging from arguments for and against including the referent as a component of the riddle to a rehashing of Köngäs Maranda's dicta on the structure of the Finnish riddle found in Layton 1976. Thus, contemporary riddle scholarship seems lodged in meta-analysis, thereby revealing a counterproductive move away from the primary object of study and toward the analysis of previous analyses of the riddle.

Such scholarship does not manifest an interest in riddling

as an activity in its own right; neither does it seem to regard the riddle as a traditional form of intrinsic cultural value. This should not be taken as a call for a moratorium on studies of the riddle as a cognitive device, but we contend that the form must be understood first as linguistic play before speculation on the genre as phenomenology in a new key can be productive. By way of redirecting the nature of riddle analysis, let us consider now an approach to the riddle genre which to this point has been little explored, namely a strict linguistic approach. The term *linguistic approach* must be limited only to those analyses that actually apply linguistic theory to the study of the riddle as language. It is this approach that we shall claim provides new insights into the fundamental nature of the riddle, and although we do not regard the works just surveyed as secondary in any sense, we shall hereafter limit our remarks to linguistic aspects of the riddle.

The first attempts at the application of linguistic theory in riddle analysis are made in Scott 1965 and 1969. In his earlier work, Scott proposes a tagmemic model for riddle analysis at the linguistic level. That is, he suggests that the riddle can be viewed as having a slot-filler structure, where various fillers (i.e., content) are inserted into the appropriate slots (i.e., the riddle structure). However, Scott is not concerned in this work with developing a linguistic approach to the riddle via tagmemics, and so he encourages others to pursue his suggestions without developing them himself.

In his later work, we find a more definite linguistic approach to the characterization of riddles. In criticizing Georges and Dundes 1963, Scott deals with the notion of topic-comment introduced there. His contention is that topic-comment is a useless tool for riddle analysis, since it has several interpretations. For instance, consider his example:

1. A blue napkin full of pears. (Sky full of clouds)

Scott claims that a traditional immediate constituent analysis of this phrase would yield a topic (or referent), *a blue napkin*, and a comment (or specification), *full of pears*. These elements correspond to the notions of referent and descriptive elements of the riddle, respectively. Scott then contends that a generative-transformational analysis of the same phrase would yield an underlying structure that looks roughly like figure 23. He correctly points out that in the case of figure 23, it is *pears* that is the subject of the underlying structure of the surface riddle. He then equates the notion of *topic* with *subject* or *subject noun phrase* (NP) and equates *comment* with *verb phrase* (VP). Thus, he claims that *pears* is part of the topic in the generative analysis, but part of the comment in the immediate constituent analysis, and that *blue napkin* is part of the comment in the generative analysis, but part of the topic in the immediate constituent analysis. Scott claims, then, that the underlying propositions of any riddle may not have the same syntactic configuration as the actual surface structure of the riddle. That is,

Figure 23

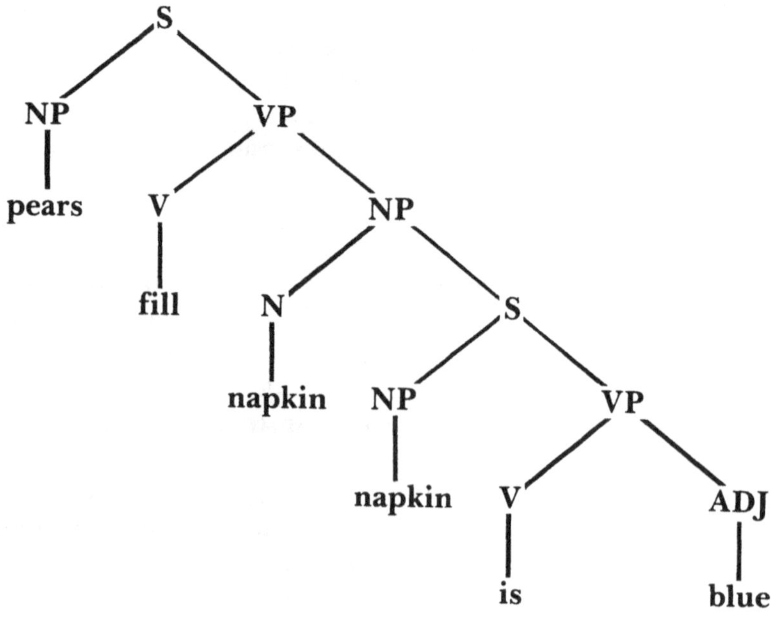

the underlying elements of the subject NP and the VP may appear in different position in the surface structure. It is Scott's contention that since topic-comment analysis yields different results at different levels, it is invalid.

Although the logic of Scott's argument is persuasive, it begins from a faulty premise. For he has incorrectly assumed that any subject, at an underlying or surface level, is to be equated with topic, and that any VP, at any level, is to be equated with comment. This is simply a misinterpretation of topic-comment analysis. For topic-comment (or to use the equivalent Prague School terminology, *theme-rheme*) is a method of analysis carried on at a syntactic level only at the surface level (see, e.g., Vachek 1970:89–92). It is designed to relate underlying *semantic* elements to their manifestations at the surface *syntactic* level. Since the effect of these semantic elements (e.g., focus) is frequently the rearranging of syntactic elements, it makes no sense to talk about topic-comment at an underlying syntactic level. In fact, since topic-comment reflects semantic relationships that affect surface syntax, Scott's phrase structure model of underlying syntactic structure is inadequate to accommodate the relationship of underlying to surface structures in riddles.

More recently, Ben-Amos 1976 attempts a brief description of linguistic ambiguity in riddles. He makes reference to two subcategories, *phonetic ambiguity* and *semantic ambiguity*. His example of the former is:

2. What's black and white and red all over? (A newspaper.)

He claims that the homophony of *red* and *read* is purely phonetic. Actually, he misses the important point that the homophony is caused by the morphology of English in this case, since the adjective *red* is homophonous with the verb *read* only when this verb exhibits its irregular past participle morpheme. Thus as we explained in chapter 3, the issue here is morphological, not phonological. Similarly, what Ben-Amos refers to as semantic ambiguity is demonstrated by him in the riddle.

3. Has eyes, cannot see. (A potato.)

He claims here that one word can refer to several objects. Again, he misses the point that the real ambiguity here is phonological, since *eye*, in all of its semantic interpretations, is pronounced the same and is the same part of speech, a noun. We might further point out that the term "semantic ambiguity" is vacuous, since all ambiguity is, by definition, semantic; the same is true of the term "phonetic ambiguity," since ambiguity results from the surface identity of two different underlying structures, as explained earlier.

Sutton-Smith 1976 sets up a classification of riddle structure based on the semantic devices employed by the riddler to confuse the riddlee. These devices involve for the most part a reclassification of semantic elements or an unexpected inversion of these elements. This analysis falls short on several counts. First, although he claims that his studies, based on children's riddles, do not for the most part fit either the systems of Georges and Dundes 1963 or of Abrahams 1968, his "reclassification" types of riddles are based purely on the same kinds of semantic oppositions discussed in those works. Second, Sutton-Smith misconstrues the term "homonym," apparently confusing it with "homograph." Specifically, he claims that the terms *hot dog* (a warm canine) and *hot dog* (a weiner) are homonyms, when in fact the pronunciations of these two phrases are distinguished in English by their stress patterns. In the latter case, primary stress is on *hot*, in the former case, on *dog*. Thus, although the two phrases are indeed spelled alike, they are not homonyms. Sutton-Smith's misinterpretation of homonyms and their potential for causing ambiguity leads him to a statement of the semantic relations in the riddle form. His conclusions, since they are based on the same sorts of observations found in Scott 1965, echo Scott's findings.

We see, then, that attempts at a linguistic characterization of the riddle have suffered primarily from misinterpretations of linguistic theory and the misapplication of theory to the riddle form. In concluding this survey of previous studies of the riddle, we must deal with a series of articles by Elli Köngäs Maranda (Maranda 1971, 1971a/1971b) that attempt to combine literary, cognitive, and linguistic analyses into an overall view of the riddle. We shall deal in some depth with her claims in the areas mentioned to determine their contributions to the study of the riddle.

From the standpoint of literary analysis, Maranda 1971 deals with metaphors in riddles. In distinguishing riddle metaphors from "ordinary" metaphors, she claims that only the latter are conventional, implying that the former are in some way unconventional. However, since a major criterion of traditional verbal art is its conventionality, both in the sense of culturally accepted formal properties and in the sense of immediate comprehensibility, one must wonder why Maranda would label as established a genre as the riddle as "unconventional" in any sense, if we mean by convention a mutual understanding about the meaning of action, which includes gestures and speech. For if riddle metaphors (or any metaphors, for that matter) were not based on accepted comparisons, answers to riddles could not be understood when they are revealed. Rather than a riddle metaphor being unconventional, then, it is the case that the metaphor contains an ambiguous element and therefore is subject to more than one conventional interpretation. Similarly, Maranda (1971a:119) claims that in offering a fresh insight the riddle must create some "hesitation." Once again, it is not the metaphor itself that offers a fresh insight or that causes the hesitation, since the metaphor exists in the riddle form and is stable as such. Rather, it is the recognition of the ambiguous element in the metaphor and its subsequent resolution that offer a fresh insight and cause hesitation.

We note here that ambiguity in the riddle may be of two sorts: linguistic or contextual (cf. Ben-Amos 1976). What we shall refer to for the time being as "contextual ambiguity" results from the fact that during the riddling act the riddlee is not aware of the specific information upon which a riddle metaphor is based. That is, whereas the agonists share a body of conventional information, only the riddler knows that, for example, eggs are being compared to houses. Therefore, the riddlee is not immediately aware of the context of the riddler's question. In this way riddles operate like non sequiturs.

All riddles manipulate context to a degree. In some, this is the only device used to create confusion. In others, however, there is no metaphorical problem at all; confusion is strictly the result of linguistic ambiguity. In such instances the block element does not have a literary basis. The block is not a result of content, but rather of the grammatical form of the riddle. In these cases we must turn to a linguistic analysis, because it is the code that is the central issue, not the message. Maranda does not distinguish between these two methods of generating confusion. We shall treat this issue in more depth in the next chapter.

Perhaps the most confusing aspect of Maranda's analysis is to be found in her transplantation of linguistic terminology into a theory of literary analysis of riddle metaphors (see especially Maranda 1971a). She sees each performance (i.e., utterance) as a unique expression of linguistic competence (1971:54). She admits, however, that in verbal art we deal with literary, not linguistic, units. Yet elsewhere in the same work she assumes that "literary units," which are left unspecified, can be fitted into a framework that corresponds terminologically with that proposed by Chomsky 1957 for linguistic units that are precisely defined. Thus, Maranda claims (1971a:124) that a given set of metaphorically related riddles have a common source. This source is her "kernel riddle," which may then be extended by means of transformations of the basic riddle and its basic metaphor.

This proposal has several drawbacks. First of all, Maranda presents the "kernel riddle," and therefore the basic metaphor of a set of riddles, as givens. We have no way of knowing why a certain riddle must be a kernel, i.e., what makes it basic. This is because Maranda ignores the fact that in the linguistic theory from which she is borrowing, kernel sentences (i.e., basic sentences from which other, related sentences may be derived) are generated by a finite set of phrase structure rules that define and limit the structure of such kernels. Maranda's system has no such check in its structure. Therefore, it does not make sense to talk about kernel riddles or basic metaphors without knowing what their natures are. Second, the notion of "transformation" as it applies to riddle metaphors is nothing more than the extension of a metaphor, e.g., extending the comparison of trees to human beings to include comparisons of tree limbs to human appendages: leaves to hair, for example. Maranda herself admits that a transformation is merely a "stretching" of a metaphor, to focus more and more on the common elements of the two sets being compared (1971:130). It is far from clear that this stretching is related in any sense to the notion of "transformation" in linguistic usage.

From a cognitive point of view, Maranda makes several questionable statements. She claims (1971b:54) that the riddle is a reciprocal genre, the proof being that the image and answer are recited by different parties participating in the riddle act. This implies that a normal riddling session is composed of a riddler, who asks questions, and one or more riddlees, who answer them. Such a situation seems unreal, since one goal of riddling is for the riddler to finally supply the answer to the riddlee(s), who has given up. So although the riddle genre may be reciprocal in some respects, Maranda's characterization of the relationship of the participants must be seriously questioned.

Maranda also makes some startling claims concerning the riddle form and metaphors. She claims, for instance, that "the riddle is put to play until all the possibilities of the image have been exhausted" (1971a:130). This implies that a riddle metaphor is carried to its logical extreme in the number of comparisons drawn from it. How we are to tell when all possible comparisons have been drawn is not specified, nor, of course, could it be in any logical sense. This statement also asks us to believe that any such comparison between two sets of elements can serve as the basis for a riddle. Such an implication is extremely suspect, as well as unverifiable.

But perhaps her most questionable claim is that people learn "riddle-making rules" just as they learn ordinary grammatical rules (1971a:136). Therefore, once we specify the riddle-making rules for a language (and so for a culture), we can predict all possible riddles in that culture, whether they exist or not. The implications here are staggering. For since Maranda sees the generation of riddles as the specification and extending of metaphors, it must follow that her riddle-making rules would serve to predict all of the possible metaphors of a culture. This in turn implies that much of the literature of a culture should be predictable, since it will rely to some degree on metaphor. The original contention and its implications are invalidated by the simple fact that to date, riddles, metaphors, and literature are ultimately unpredictable in all cultures. Likewise, Maranda's claim that nonoccurring riddles that are predicted by her riddle-making rules must be considered as real riddles of a culture is invalidated by the fact that not all metaphors serve as the basis for riddles.

As pointed out above, Maranda's basic error is in considering the metaphor itself to be the prime concern of riddle analysis. We have seen, to the contrary, that it is not the metaphor alone, but the obscuring of some element of the metaphor that is central to such studies. Such concerns as riddle- or metaphor-making rules are not primary issues, in a real sense, since the central problem of explaining the riddle is in defining its enigmatic nature. The rigorous linguistic treatment of riddles we have proposed serves to clarify this enigmatic nature, at least for a certain category of riddles.

It is this linguistic characterization of the riddle form that both reaffirms the basic definition of the riddle and provides the means to more clearly delineate this form in a performance context. For we find that most scholars agree that a riddle consists of both a question and an answer. This two-part structure creates the pattern of tension and release that makes it possible to see the riddle as a paradigm of many of our other aesthetic interactions.

As far as we can determine, riddles do not exist as unanswered questions in any traditions, and certainly not in English-speaking traditions. The riddle's interrogative format militates against such an eventuality, and the tensions generated by the lack of closure in unanswered questions makes this intolerable. Even the Koan, a related form based on the question and answer model, is seen to produce intolerable tension until resolved. (See Zug 1967). Thus, we shall refer to the "riddle" as designating both a question and its answer, rather than, as some scholars have done, referring to the riddle as a question that is somehow analyzable apart from its answer (e.g., Georges and Dundes 1963). If we intend to discuss traditional verbal art, we must turn to the tradition-bearers for our data. There is no exception to the rule that in its natural context the riddle question is either solved (i.e., provided with an appropriate answer by the riddlee) or revealed (i.e., provided with an appropriate answer by the riddler).

If we seem to belabor the issue that riddles are formally conventional questions and answers, it is due to the fact that the scholarship has led us away from this rather obvious conclusion by adhering to a notion of "true riddles." Taylor 1943 and 1951, drawing on Meier 1901, who drew first upon Novakovic 1877, characterized the true riddle as a riddle that "compares an object to another entirely different object" (1943:129) and subsequently as a description "in terms intended to suggest something entirely different" (1951:2). Beyond the criticism that one might use essentially the same definition for metaphor or proverb, one must wonder what makes such riddles more "true" than other verbal enigmas. If we wish to deal with riddles as traditional oral phenomena, then, the literary origin of the term "true riddle" should arouse our suspicions. Moreover, this notion seems burdened by unwarranted preconceptions and, therefore, incompatible with the dispassionate ideals of scholarly investigation.

Let us pursue this last claim a bit. We find that in riddles, the question format prevails even though a specific riddle may be framed in a conventional form that does not on the surface level appear to be interrogative. For example, "Mr. Blackman was going to town; him drop him kerchief an' couldn't pick it up (Crow drops a feather) (Taylor 1951:265)" appears to be a descriptive statement. We must, however, be cognizant of the fact that this statement is uttered in a specific context. The group's accumulated experience with similar forms on similar occasions (i.e., its tradition) demands that this descriptive statement be answered. Therefore, it functions interrogatively within a particular tradition.

As indicated above, a preoccupation with the outward structure of such texts and the consequent deemphasis of context has misled some commentators on the riddle. What is essential to making the preceding example a riddle is not description. "A rolling stone gathers no moss" is also descriptive. However, as we recognize by virtue of a shared tradition, this is not a riddle, but a proverb, a conventional solution to a recurrent social problem. An essential criterion for defining the riddle, then, is a traditionally conceptualized interrogative format, whether the interrogation is manifested on a surface level or not.

A more fundamental order of definition is obviously in order here. We therefore suggest that riddles are not simply descriptions whose referents must be guessed or revealed, but are conventional questions of various sorts that must be answered. Given this primary criterion, we argue that enigmatic questions and answers like "When is coffee like the soil? When it is ground." are no less "true riddles" than those given by Taylor. Although the present example is based on a cause-and-effect rather than a descriptive model, it falls within our interrogative format, is transmitted orally (like the majority of riddles), and is included in the riddle category by informants.

We do not insist, however, that all traditional interrogative forms should be considered folk riddles. There are many oral traditions based on the question and answer format whose solutions require the recall of esoteric facts rather than the exercise of wit. Whereas it is impossible to create an exhaustive list of nonriddle questions and answers, the following categories suggest forms that, for various reasons, should be excluded from the riddle genre. Indeed, as pointed out in Jones and Hawes 1972, the folk often supply criteria, either implicit or explicit, for excluding certain question and answer forms from the riddle category.

The catechetical questions that are often incorporated into ritual or initiation are not, strictly speaking, solvable. They actually operate like statements. That is, the answers are actually learned as bodies of doctrine that, on prescribed occasions, are elicited through questions that demand an automatic response rather than a thoughtful solution (i.e., the exercise of wit).

Zen *koan*, since they contain descriptive elements and a referent that must be guessed, are considered riddles by Zug 1967. According to the criterion of solvability stated above, however, this form should be seen as a special variety of catechetical question. Zug, in fact, points out the form's organic relationship to the Chinese *mondo*, which is strictly a catechetical form. Of utmost importance is the fact that the tension arising from attempting to logically solve the *koan* forces the questioned party to *satori*, an altered state of perception, rather than to a solution in our terms. The *koan*, then, is unsolvable in the sense that solvability is conceived in this study, and so is a nonriddle.

Clever questions or wisdom questions also depend upon a command of special bodies of knowledge, e.g., baseball, mathematics, or the Bible. Since these verbal enigmas require only recall and not the exercise of wit, they cannot be solved from the information supplied by the question, and are not properly considered riddles, either.

The "neck riddle" calls for perhaps the most esoteric knowledge of all, for its "solution" depends upon knowledge of a unique, personal episode. Most of these riddles are contained within traditional narratives concerning a condemned prisoner who poses a riddle that his executioners cannot solve, and who, by virtue of his cleverness, "saves his neck." Not all neck riddles, however, deal with such life and death situations. For example, the Biblical Samson employs the form for a wager rather than as a life-saving measure in Judg. 14:5–9. In addition to its unsolvability, the neck riddle's narrative context prohibits its inclusion in the riddle category. This latter circumstance is especially critical, since it indicates that this form is generally conceived of as a narrative episode and therefore is not available for inclusion in a socially defined riddling context (cf. Abrahams 1972:183–86).

The joking question or riddle joke merits consideration, since it mimics or parodies the riddle and is often the sort of verbal enigma volunteered as a riddle by urban American informants, both in riddle sessions and during more artificial elicitation. These questions should be excluded from our formally defined riddle category because the referents of most of them (especially cyclical forms such as Little Moron, Elephant, Grape, or ethnic-oriented items) are so tenuously connected to their questions as to be unsolvable. They thus block any exercise of wit in the sense being used here. Joking questions, then, do not operate as riddles at all, but simply as devices that allow the performer to deliver a punchline. Therefore, no degree of familiarity with "elephant jokes" would provide the riddlee with the ability to provide the answer "So he can hide in a cherry tree" to the question "Why does an elephant paint his toenails red?"

Let us turn now from our discussion of what riddles are not and summarize the attributes of the folk riddle as we have outlined them. We see first that the riddle form is based on the question and answer format. Moreover, it is potentially solvable from the information included in the question if the riddlee is able to determine the witty devices for confusion employed to frame the riddle. In turn, we see that the information necessary to discern the witty devices is to be found entirely by virtue of participation in a cultural system (i.e., shared language, world view, and tropes). Finally, the riddle act must, like all folklore, have a conventional locus within a particular tradition and within a performance context.

Characterizing the riddle in this fashion effectively eliminates the major problems inherent in previous definitions of the genre. First, it limits the domain of the genre to a specific type of performance involving definable strategies that can be stated and thus compared across genres. In addition, we have a means for contrastive classification of the other question-and-answer sequences we have just discussed.

Thus it is not our intention to exclude from consideration performances such as neck-riddles or riddle parodies that may occur in riddling questions. Rather, it is our intention to facilitate a more precise explanation of such performances by pointing out that they differ in significant ways from the riddles that form the basis of our analysis. In this way we seek to provide an analysis that may serve as a base for further study and avoid one that, in attempting to encompass too much, is reduced to a series of ad hoc statements.

Second, our definition clearly establishes the folk riddle as language, as well as literature. The agonistic armature of the riddle and the oral properties that frequently have been ignored in previous studies are placed in proper perspective. Moreover, our definition underscores the fact that the riddling contest involves not only "wits" (cleverness), but wit (artful devices for the creation of confusion). Also, with the notion of a conventional locus, this definition goes beyond mere surface structure to note that although some riddles look like statements, they are intended to be interpreted as questions. Therefore, this definition of the riddle argues for examining riddles in context as speech acts rather than in isolation as texts. This principle is critical when attempting to determine solvability, interrogative qualities, and social function. The proposed set of criteria reflects more accurately riddles in their "natural state" and is free from the preconceptions upon which the bulk of previous scholarship rests.

METAPHORICAL AMBIGUITY

Chapter Six

WE HAVE NOW EXAMINED in some depth the formal linguistic properties that are exploited in the riddle genre and thereby become part of the definition of wit. We have shown that the exploitation of formal properties of language represents a continuum of strategies from those that depend upon oral transmission to those that must be written to achieve their effect. This continuum thus takes into account the major manifestations of language and points out the nature of the relationship between these manifestations. The delineation of this continuum has emphasized our preoccupation with the relationship of form to content in the various exploitations of flexible areas within the formal code to produce licensed confusion in the message.

We turn now to the characterization of another continuum. In this case, we are concerned with the differing natures of riddles like 1–3 and those in 4 and 5.

1. What turns but never moves? *Milk.*
2. What's black and white and red (read) all over? *A newspaper.*
3. How is a duck like an icicle? *Both grow down.*
4. In spring I am gay
   In handsome array;
   In summer more clothing I wear;
   When colder it grows

I fling off my clothes;
And in winter I quite naked appear. *A tree.*

5. I have a cock on yonder hill
I keep him for a wonder.
And every time the cock do crow,
It lightens, hails and thunders. *A gun.*

We shall define the difference in strategies used to create a block element in these riddles as one of formal grammatical ambiguity of the type already discussed (and exampled here in 1–3) versus literary or metaphorical ambiguity, i.e., ambiguity resulting from cultural tropes that produce, in the riddling context, surprising additional semantic structures for existing words or phrases.

Further, we shall claim that the two types of ambiguity that we distinguish represent endpoints on a continuum of the conscious, artful manipulation of ambiguous language in verbal play, and we shall examine various points along this continuum that fit neither extreme exactly, but that exhibit elements of both. We shall see, then, how the relationship between grammatical and metaphorical ambiguity defines a continuum of ambiguity, and we shall suggest how it is that we can categorize various types of ambiguity in the riddle genre.

Having already paid close attention to the nature of grammatical ambiguity, let us turn to an examination of metaphor and metaphorical ambiguity as language and as a strategy in riddling. The study of metaphor has a long literary tradition. Folklore, though a relatively new discipline, has also demonstrated a concern with figurative language in oral tradition (Taylor 1943 and 1951 being the best examples). Until fairly recently, however, metaphor has not been the subject of extensive treatment by linguists. Because our arguments are based on the assertion that the code is the central issue in ridding, and linguistics is the discipline most directly concerned with the code, this recent scholarship, though lacking in some regards, is central to our understanding of those riddles that employ metaphor as a block element.

A review of linguistic literature on metaphor (e.g., Bickerton 1969, Mooij 1976) shows that metaphors have been categorized largely on the basis of grammatical and semantic deviance, from the linguistic point of view. Let us consider a linguistic analysis of the following examples.

6. Women and men went their came.
7. Hate blows a bubble of despair.

In the first example, we find syntactic deviance in two respects. First, the verb *went* is intransitive and therefore should not take a direct object. Second, even if *went* were transitive and so could take a direct object, direct objects must be noun phrases, and *came*, which is in direct object position in this sentence, is clearly not a noun phrase, but a verb. A componential analysis of this utterance yields the following scheme for the crucial terms *went* and *came*:

went = [+ verb, - transitive, + past . . .]
came = [+ verb, - transitive, + past . . .]

This analysis shows in terms of a binary feature system the specific features of these terms that conflict to produce syntactic anomaly.

In the second example, the syntax of the construction is grammatical, but the semantics of the sentence is anomalous. *Hate*, which is an abstract, inanimate noun, cannot serve as the subject of *blow*, which requires an animate, concrete, living subject. Moreover, *bubble*, which is a concrete noun, cannot be described as being composed of *despair*, since *despair* is not concrete. Again, we can display the conflicting features of the relevant elements in the diagrammatic fashion:

hate = [+ noun, - animate, - concrete . . .]
blow = [+ verb, + transitive, + animate subject . . .]
bubble = [+ noun, + concrete, - animate . . .]
despair = [+ noun, - concrete, - animate . . .]

Obviously, the type of analysis just mentioned is concerned with figurative usage of language vis à vis literal usage, and the interplay of literal and figurative usage is basic to this analysis. Such analyses, however, focus on contrastive aspects of the two usages, rather than on the nature of the relationship between the two. The understanding and description by formalized procedures of this relationship is crucial to understanding riddle construction and the means by which this genre exploits linguistic malleability in both grammatically ambiguous and metaphorical riddles.

In a recent work dealing with children's riddling, McDowell 1979 addresses the roles of metaphor and ambiguity in the strategy of riddling in general. Through a discussion of the notions of homophony and polysemy, he attempts to construct a theoretical base for explaining how riddles may be used to reify what he terms "dead words" or "dead metaphors," through the resurrection of literal meaning. Although his effort to present a unified approach to both metaphorical and formally ambiguous riddles is commendable, when McDowell's notions are examined from a linguistic point of view we discover that his basic assumptions concerning the relationship of linguistic ambiguity and imagery in riddles are questionable, and the resulting framework he constructs is neither linguistically nor psychologically valid. Before suggesting a more appropriate means of characterizing the relationship between linguistic ambiguity and metaphorical language, these assertions concerning the flaws in McDowell's scheme require clarification.

McDowell bases his arguments on that segment of verbal art he has labeled the *interrogative ludic routine*, which he defines as "an extrasentential verbal sequence founded on the interrogative system of the language, but adapting that system to purposes of play" (1979:ix). Though not inconsistent with the concept of the riddle we have advanced in this work, McDowell intends by this notion to encompass a wider range of materials than the riddle genre proper. We shall concern ourselves only with the relevance of his comments to traditional riddling.

McDowell sets forth in chapter five of his book a typology of "ludic transformations" or devices for deceiving a riddlee, using either a linguistic code or a cognitive code. Concentrating on those devices that exploit the linguistic code, we find two basic types of ludic transformation employed in the interrogative ludic routine that includes riddles. The first type operates through the juxtaposition of contradictory elements in such a way as to facilitate the perception of an anomaly. This strategy, McDowell claims, is realized in riddles by use of homophony, the exploitation of a single phonetic string that may represent two or more semantic interpretations. His examples of this type of riddle include:

8. What's black and white and red/read all over? *A newspaper.*
9. What has four wheels and flies? *A garbage truck.*

The second type of ludic transformation depends on a comparison, a transitory association of two similar elements in such a way as to highlight the perception of congruence. This strategy is realized through what McDowell terms "conventional polysemy," the historically or psychologically motivated occurrence of two or more semantic interpretations in a single phonetic string. Thus polysemy differs from homophony by a factor of motivation. An example of a polysemous riddle is:

10. Something has an ear and cannot hear. *Corn.*

Another sort of comparison, radical polysemy, is seen in riddles such as:

11. A thousand lights in a dish. *Stars.*

McDowell (1979:101) contends, "In taking up radical polysemy we depart from those comparisons enfranchised in ordinary usage." The strategy requires the linking of two *relata* "without the prior sanction of conventional usage," and "involves the transitory association of two objects on the basis of some common feature." Although McDowell suggests various syntagmatic relations between signifier and signified, it is sufficient to note that figurative usage is the common base of such riddles.

Let us examine the typology in some detail. In the case of homophony, McDowell suggests that the cause of homophony is the conflict between restrictions on the phonemic inventories of languages (i.e., possible sounds in natural languages) and the "fundamental logic of natural languages," which "includes a one-to-one correspondence between phonetic representation and semantic representation" (1979:90). In the same discussion he considers this conflict (which he calls "wrinkles in the code") to "constitute a threat to the very possibility of language," which necessitates disambiguation of homophonous elements, usually through context. It is the manipulation of these "wrinkles in the code" that are the focus of riddles like 1 and 2.

McDowell is correct in assessing the role of homophony in riddling, but we must take issue with his statement concerning the place of homophony in language and thus with his treatment of homophony in general. First, and most important, homophony is not a "threat" to language, but rather a manifestation of one very important aspect of natural languages, namely redundancy.

By redundancy we do not mean "needlessly repetitive" in the nontechnical sense, but rather we mark the usage as it applies to language as a system of communication. Let us examine this notion briefly and see how homophony can be treated as a form of redundancy.

Natural languages (i.e., those spoken by humans) constitute a subset of communications systems in general, e.g., systems like Morse code, signal flags, or computer languages. If we view such systems as consisting of a source, a signal, and a receiver, we can see language as a system that can be schematized as in figure 24. Thus, a message (information) is encoded according to some set of signals and is transmitted over a channel to a receiver where the signals are decoded to reveal the message. In spoken language the information source is the human brain, the transmitter is

Figure 24

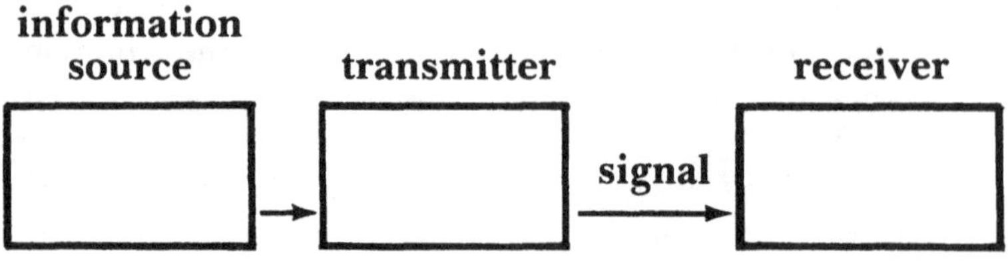

the vocal tract, the signals are phonemes, the channel is vibrating air, and the receiver is another human being.

Ideal communication in all communications systems is achieved when the minimum number of signals possible to send any given message is used. For example, if one were using a transmitter code in which the signals were the presence or absence of a flow of electric current, one could encode the message "yes" by allowing the current to flow, and "no" by stopping the flow. Thus the two positions of a simple relay, open or closed, could correspond to the two messages. Such a system, however, is subject to outside interference with the channel. That is, although the intended message may be properly encoded, the channel may be disturbed, in the case at hand, for example, by static in the system or by a temporary interruption in the flow of the current. Such unintended outside interference is termed *noise* in communication theory. Noise may cause the signal, and hence the message, to become garbled or even changed completely. Thus, any communication system that is subject to noise must make provision to ensure effective transmission of messages.

Redundancy is such a provision. We may define redundancy with Rosie 1973 as "the presence of any detail in a . . . system, other than the minimum necessary for the representation or transmission of the required information" (1973:60). The simplest example of redundancy in any system is the repetition of a signal. This method is, of course, used in natural languages. However, the amount of information transmitted by natural languages is in general far too great for the systems of signals used to transmit this information. English, for example, has approximately thirty-six phonemes with which to encode an infinite number of messages. Clearly the burden on the phonemic system is enormous. Thus, many messages that are encoded are very similar to one another, often varying by only one signal (i.e., phoneme). If we consider the word level, for instance, we find many words that differ by only one phoneme (called *minimal pairs*):

bat	/bæt/
cat	/kæt/
hat	/hæt/
mat	/mæt/

Such distinctions make effective use of the phoneme inventory of English. However, human communication is subject to noise from many sources, for example, other people talking, coughing, traffic, howling wind, which makes the perception of such distinctions in the system difficult. Thus, English, as all natural languages, has redundancy factors built into the system.

One such factor is the set of restrictions on initial consonant clusters in English. Thus, no word in English may begin with a cluster of more than three consonants, and then only if the first one is /s/. Further, if the first consonant in a triconsonantal initial cluster is /s/, the second consonant can only be /t/, /p/, or /k/, and the third only /r/, or /l/. Obviously, these combinations represent only a minute subset of the logically possible initial consonant clusters in English, given the entire phonemic inventory. These limitations, however, enable the receiver of a message encoded in English phonemes to decode the message even if his reception of the message is partially obscured. Since the number of possible combinations of phonemes is restricted, the receiver, who is aware of these restrictions, is able to guess fairly accurately what a given phoneme in a given sequence of phonemes might reasonably be. Another clue to the decoding of such a message is the context, to which we shall return momentarily.

Another manifestation of redundancy is homophony. In this instance different messages have identical phonemic representation. McDowell, as we saw, sees this situation as antithetical to the one-to-one correspondence of phonetic representation to semantic representation that he assumes. However, his assumption does not in fact hold for natural languages; although an ideal communication system, one that is not subject to noise, could have a one-to-one correspondence of signal to message, such a situation is obviously impossible in natural languages. The basic reason is one of limitation of the human brain. Simply, it would be impossible for humans to store in memory or to discriminate the number of messages required for such a system without overlap of signals. Further, a one-to-one correspondence of the type McDowell sees as basic to language would be impractical, since any interference (noise) within the transmission of reception of a message would render the message unintelligible; without built-in restrictions on the system there would be no way for a receiver of a message to guess what the garbled part of a message might be.

Thus, homophony (and hence ambiguity) is a result of the limits on the possible number of combinations of signals used to encode messages. It is not a "threat" to language, but rather is basic to the function of language as a communication system. The "threat" posed by riddles is to the usual interaction of speakers in normal discourse; it is caused by the exploitation of ambiguity or tropes inherent in linguistic structures or in the comparisons of cultural categories. The linguistic or broader cultural elements found in riddles are not themselves in danger of being "turned on their head" (McDowell, 1979:208); rather, the threat of disorder is at the level of interaction. That is, riddles take the question-and-answer format of normal interaction and play on this conventional mode of exchanging information. In this way riddles are a threat to the communicative frame, since, among other considerations, the riddlee must determine whether the interaction mode is serious or playful (see Bateson 1972:177ff).

McDowell's discussion does, nonetheless, raise the interesting question of how we deal with the potential problems inherent in homophony, the foremost among these being the perception of which semantic representation a source intends when sending a message that contains homophonous, and therefore ambiguous, elements. The answer is that the receiver appeals to the broader level of discourse and the clues provided therein to ascertain the context of the ambiguous element in a given utterance, thereby eliminating certain semantic interpretations as possible intended messages. Recourse to context in discourse is often sufficient to resolve such ambiguity. If not, then elaboration, i.e., messages that serve to define and clarify other messages, is required.

Let us turn now to the cases of homophonic riddles cited by McDowell, both of which he claims turn on the juxtaposition of two possible interpretations of a single word. Thus in riddle 8 we have the simple adjective *red* juxtaposed with the past participle *read*, and in riddle 9, the word *flies* is either a plural noun or a third person singular present tense verb. However, although McDowell's analysis may be adequate at a surface taxonomic level, it will not suffice if he is to fulfill his goals of relating surface patterns to underlying deep linguistic structures (1979:59). For indeed, these two riddles are examples of only two of many "wrinkles" in the linguistic code that are exploited in riddling, and most important, their sources are entirely different.

Riddle 8 falls into the category of morphological riddles defined in chapter 3, whereby the homophony involved depends crucially on a peculiarity of English morphology, namely that the verb *read* /riyd/ plus its past participle morpheme, are pronounced /rɛd/. Riddle 9, as McDowell sees, depends on syntax, but he misses the point that the ambiguity in 9 arises from the nature of the deletion transformations involved in producing homophonous surface pronunciations from two different underlying structures, rather than from a case where a "kernel element, consisting of a linguistic unit with homophonic properties, is embedded within a syntactic structure and semantic argument in such a manner as to enhance the perception of ambiguity" (1979:93).

This latter view confuses underlying structure, surface structure, and the syntactic transformations that link the two. From a linguistic point of view, we are clearly dealing with two kernel elements, i.e., the underlying structures of the two semantic readings employed in the riddle, not one, as McDowell claims. Further, it is not the kernels themselves but their eventual surface structures that have homophonous properties. Homophony results from the grammatical rule that allows deletion of repeated elements, so that the following schema applies, where brackets indicate material that has been deleted.

12. What has four wheels and what flies?
    What has four wheels and [ ] flies?
13. What has four wheels and what has flies?
    What has four wheels and [ ] flies?

Nor can we say that any linguistic unit is embedded in a syntactic structure or a semantic argument. Rather, two semantic arguments (more properly, semantic propositions) are made to coincide in syntactic form by exploiting formal grammatical processes. McDowell's observations do not draw this important line of development. They confuse the properties of the *message* (semantics) with manipulations of the *signal* (grammar). It is the identification and classification of the syntactic transformations like those involved in riddle 9 that is vital to an understanding of the linguistic strategy involved in such riddles.

McDowell's second type of ludic transformation, which depends upon comparison, draws force from what he calls "conventional polysemy." As stated, this involves an historical or psychological motivation for establishing a relationship between two otherwise homophonous items. In homophony proper for McDowell, the two or more semantic interpretations which may derive from a given phonetic string do so fortuitously. He raises two main points in this connection. The first deals with the problems of distinguishing homophony from polysemy. The second deals with polysemy as it occurs in everyday language and as it occurs in the riddle genre.

In regard to the first point, McDowell allows that homophony and polysemy seem to blend in some cases. For instance, he considers the homophonous pair *ear* (organ of hearing) and *ear* (head of corn), which have different etymologies and so are not historically related. He claims that in riddles like 10, which also turns on the word *ear*, we have polysemy, in that there is an "intuitive perception of a semantic relationship between the two lexemes coincident on the phonetic base *ear*" (1979:96). He continues, "Even awareness of the actual historical picture cannot shake our determination to hear a polysemic relationship in our duplicitous phonetic sequence. The intuitions of native speakers will then serve as the technique for sorting out homophony from polysemy . . . Admittedly, marginal cases are difficult to classify but the majority of the corpus falls easily into one category or the other" (1979:96).

There are two major problems with this distinction between homophony and polysemy. The first is that McDowell assumes that the native speaker's intuition is sufficient in deciding whether a given instance is a case of homophony or polysemy. This problem of whether given homophones are somehow related is one that has not eluded semanticists from the time of the ancient Greeks. In the modern linguistic era, this problem has been treated by among other schools, structuralist morphology, and general semantics.[1] Simply, it is the case that native intuitions in instances like *ear* vary drastically.

McDowell himself proves this by insisting that *ear* is (for him) polysemous, but admitting that in fact the two words pronounced /iyr/ are not historically related. By his own definitions, the two words should be homophonous, not polysemous. Another parallel case is seen in the instance of the word(s) *board* (plank), *board* (council), and *board* (meals). Historically, we see a development from *board* designating a plank of wood to the specialization of the plank in its use as a table for meetings of councils and for eating meals. These specializations develop in turn to designate the people at the table in the former instance and the activity at the table in the latter instance.

There is no way to predict whether native speakers of English will, when asked, perceive any semantic (or historical) relationship between these uses of the word *board*. By McDowell's definitions, *board* must be polysemous. What, then, are we to say about the native speakers who see no apparent relationship between the uses, and who thus see the uses as instances of what McDowell terms homophony? Clearly, as native speakers, their intuitions cannot be "wrong." They simply have a different lexical entry in their mental lexicon for *board* than do native speakers who perceive a relationship in the uses. Thus one cannot, as McDowell does, gloss over such problems for his theory by appeal to intuition. On the one hand, he admits that intuition is sometimes at variance with etymology; on the other hand, psychological aspects of intuition may vary drastically from person to person. As stated by Lyons 1969, "The distinction between homonymy [homophony] and multiple meaning [polysemy] is, in the last resort, indeterminant and arbitrary" (1969:406). Lyons further states that evidence of this arbitrariness can be found reflected in discrepancies of classifications in dictionaries, where lexicographers must decide whether two homophonous words are separate but homophonous or merely polysemous.

The second flaw in McDowell's distinction between homophony and polysemy is that he considers the etymology of a word, its history, to be relevant to making this distinction in contemporary usage. This approach suffers two drawbacks. First, it lays the burden of the history of a language on every speaker of that language. As Lyons (1969:407) points out in this regard, "Any historical knowledge we might have about the development of the meanings of words is in principle irrelevant to their synchronic use and interpretation." Indeed, as Lyons states, this must be true, unless it were discovered that people who are familiar with the history of the language use it differently from those who are not. Simply put, to claim that words are historical entities is to belabor the obvious. Explanations of synchronic usage in terms of historical usage are irrelevant, since the histories of words are not part of the synchronic grammar of a language and thus do not affect the strictly synchronic usage involved in riddles (see de Saussure 1922).

Further, McDowell himself demonstrates that historical considerations are tenuous grounds upon which to judge homophony from polysemy, since he admits that other considerations, like his own insistence on a psychological link between the two meanings of *ear* discussed above, may do "some violence to etymological reality." Thus the distinction between homophony and polysemy is seen not only to be untenable in view of previous work in the field, but in fact in large part irrelevant to the type of ambiguity present in riddles.

Let us turn now to McDowell's treatment of conventional polysemy in everyday life and as it appears in riddling. McDowell defines conventional polysemy as "precisely those instances of polysemy which are codified in daily use of a language. They may at one time have been productive of surprise, but in current usage they have become as regular as any other lexemes encountered in the language" (1979:96). He further claims that the ludic transformation of, for example, riddles juxtaposes current linguistic usage with alternate hearings derived from an historical act of comparison. As examples of this strategy he gives the following routines, which for his purposes are classified as riddles.

14. What did the rug say to the floor? *I've got you covered.*
15. What did the wall say to the other wall? *Meet you at the corner.*

Clearly, to claim that these riddles are polysemous in nature based on historical considerations is subject to the criticism just presented. However, McDowell makes a further claim for such routines, that they take automatized language (i.e., familiar phrases, clichés, idioms) and revitalize them by forcing a reinterpretation of this language. Thus he says that riddles breathe "life into dead words" by allowing for an "unconventional reading" of these words (1979:97–98). In the two examples cited, one is hard put to discern any unconventional reading in either case. In the first, we find homophony of a literal use of the phrase *got you covered* with an idiomatic use of the same phrase. The contrastive use of homophonous phrases, although it constitutes a block element, can hardly be said to "breathe life" into either usage, nor can either be termed "unconventional," since both are in current usage. This is even more true in the second example, since we are merely presented with contrastive readings (both current) of the word *corner.*

In this same vein, McDowell cites Sapir 1977 in claiming that riddles may bring old sayings to life to literalize a dead metaphor. His first examples in this regard are:

16. Why does time fly? *Cause people are always trying to kill it.*
17. Why did the boy throw the clock out of the window? *To see time fly.*

He correctly sees that these riddles play on the literal vs. the figurative meaning of the phrases *time flies* and *to kill time*, but to claim that "in this manner old language is invested with new life" (1979:99) is again to confuse diachrony with synchrony. Regardless of the time depth for the figurative meanings involved, these ludic routines play on two synchronic meanings of the phrase involved, one a literal reading, the other a frozen, idiomatic reading. Historical considerations are irrelevant.

This point is reinforced if we look at further examples that McDowell claims demonstrate the resuscitation of metaphor, and thus a revival of old language:

18. What has an eye but cannot see? *Potato.*
19. What has a tongue and can't talk? *Shoe.*
20. What has teeth but cannot eat? *Saw.*

Again, although these riddles may be based historically on earlier comparisons, the formal, grammatical ambiguities in the words *eye*, *tongue*, and *teeth* exist synchronically, and must exist synchronically for the riddles to work. Further, it is disputable whether *eye* in riddle 18 is to be considered metaphorical, or merely homophonous on its two readings. That is, it may be argued that the images involved in *tongue* and *teeth* are still synchronically retrievable, but the comparison that renders a human eye and the tuber of a potato similar seems to be weaker, synchronically, and is evident primarily because of the juxtaposition with the verb *see*. This example either has passed, or is in the process of passing, from the realm of metaphor to that of homophony, or formal linguistic ambiguity. The same is true of riddles like:

21. Where is the smallest bridge in the world? *On your nose.*
22. What has a bed but never sleeps? *A river.*

These riddles, although they may be intuited as being at least semimetaphorical, are clearly not so well grounded in imagery as riddles like 19 and 20.

In riddle 21, the use of *bridge* to describe the upper part of the nose, first found in English around 1450, may be claimed to be metaphorical usage, but as such is in need of explanation. For this reason it may be claimed as easily that the two senses of *bridge* are instances of homophonous words, rather than of metaphorical extension of meaning. Indeed, as was the case with *board*, native speaker intuitions vary as to the status of the two meanings of *bridge* being discussed.

In riddle 22 we see a similar case involving the word *bed*. Although the use of *bed* to mean the bottom of a river is clearly metaphorical in origin, it is dubious whether in current usage the relationship between the sleeping place and the river bottom is anything other than simple lexical ambiguity or homophony. Again, though reflection may result in a native speaker's being able to reconstruct the original metaphor (or sometimes to propose an incorrect folk-etymology), the figurative nature of *bed* meaning "river bottom" is clearly not as strong as the metaphors in examples utilizing *tongue* and *teeth* cited above. What we are suggesting, then, is that some figurative language is more figurative than other, and that metaphor may pass gradually from the realm of figurative language to the realm of formal ambiguity, i.e., pure homophony, of the type seen in examples like:

23. What lock can no key open? *A lock of hair.*

24. What vegetable is unpopular on ships? *A leek.*

Here no imagery is involved at all. McDowell has classified this latter type as distinct from those in examples 18–22 and has assumed that 18–22 are of a single type. Let us now examine this assumption, and so the entire scheme of classification of riddles by type of image and/or ambiguity.

McDowell's distinctions between homophony and polysemy have been shown to be untenable both theoretically and practically. Similarly, his claims concerning the resurrection of dead metaphors by the resurrection of their literal meanings ignores a crucial element. Specifically, there is no need to "resurrect" the literal meaning of a metaphor (or idiom, or any figure of speech) in the riddle context since it is this literal meaning that is the base for the riddle metaphor in the first place. Thus, the literal meaning is a constant. It is the figurative meaning that is subject to changes, e.g., the automatization of meaning, or the freezing of syntactic form. What McDowell sees as a revitalization of an image vis à vis its literal interpretation is often merely a synchronic exploitation of an idiomatic phrase vis à vis a literal meaning of that phrase.

The importance of McDowell's work is that it endeavors to come to terms with the important matter of linguistic vis à vis metaphorical wit in riddles. This is the central issue in riddle construction. His work also presents an array of riddles, some clearly homophonous, some clearly metaphorical, and some that fit neither category exactly. As we have seen, neither McDowell's theory nor native speaker intuitions are sufficient to classify the range of riddles and ludic routines he treats. The problem is attributable, in part, to his tendency to force data into rigid categories. The notions of anomaly vs. congruence exemplify this problem. Rather than existing in polar opposition, it is obvious that the two qualities must coexist within riddles; anomaly characteristically serves as a block element, but congruence must emerge for the answer to be apt. In the riddle, "What's black and white and red/read all over?" for example, the physical anomaly of color forestalls solution, but ultimately gives way to the congruence of the adjective *red* with the past participle *read* at the level of utterance. Turning to metaphorical riddles we see the same pattern. Take, for example, our number 4:

> In spring I am gay
> In handsome array;
> In summer more clothing I wear;
> When colder it grows,
> I fling off my clothes;
> And in winter I quite naked appear. *A tree.*

The anomalous shedding of "garments" with the onset of cold weather becomes congruous with revelation of the figurative qualities of description. Fundamentally, McDowell does not realize, as has been suggested above, that the distinction between the type of ambiguity that is purely formal (homophony) and the type that relies on metaphor is not a strict categorical distinction, but rather is a continuum of ambiguity that ranges from the literary to the formal grammatical types that have been discussed.

It is the element of ambiguity that permeates all of the riddle categories we have examined and that serves to relate them. If we begin from the general concept of ambiguity, it becomes apparent how the variety of riddles in current use in our culture fall into a gradient classification. Certainly the relationship between metaphor and ambiguity has not escaped treatment in the relevant literature. Perhaps the first direct treatment of this relationship is to be found in William Empson's work, *Seven Types of Ambiguity*. Although Empson lacks the linguistic framework necessary to define the formal aspects of metaphorical, or literary ambiguity, he rightly sees metaphor as properly ambiguous; it has both literal and figurative senses. Leech 1966 has discussed metaphor similarly as a type of ambiguity at the "referential semantic level."

In terms of the types of ambiguity relevant for riddle analysis discussed thus far, metaphor represents ambiguity at the lexical, or word/sound level. As we have shown, surface homophony may be the result of processes that occur at the phonological, morphological, or syntactic level of grammar. Thus metaphor is lexical in nature, since it represents a situation whereby an additional semantic underlying structure is created for an existing word or phrase.

However, literary or metaphorical ambiguity goes beyond the simple type of lexical ambiguity we demonstrated in analyzing the sentence *John lives near the bank*. As Leech points out, a figurative or metaphorical item "has been given referential meaning outside of its normal range of meanings . . . by the standards of the accepted code (i.e., literal meaning) a literary metaphor is a semantic absurdity" (1966:147,149). He offers the example *Some books are to be tasted, others to be swallowed, and some few to be chewed and digested* (Bacon, "Of Studies"). Such imagery, as noted at the beginning of this chapter, has been treated linguistically primarily in terms of deviance, as a type of language that violates certain grammatical or semantic norms of ordinary speech. If we take another perspective, however, namely that of metaphor as contrived ambiguity, we may partially characterize metaphor in its proper context as a form that is closely related to ambiguous utterances in normal, utilitarian speech, and which thus draws directly on "ordinary" grammar for its creativity, and which, indeed, frequently passes out of literary usage and becomes an element of ordinary speech.

Let us now consider this last point in more depth. It is clear that metaphor is an extension of the phenomenon of ambiguity or homophony in ordinary speech. In ordinary speech grammatical ambiguity is inherently resolvable at the level of contextual discourse. This aspect of normal communication channels may be consciously inverted, and thus intensified, to create ambiguity in a performance context, as discussed above. Metaphor may be considered as taking this type of intensification a step further. Although ambiguity in both normal speech and riddling may derive from formal grammatical ambiguity, metaphorical ambiguity depends upon more general cognitive associations or analogies between the literal and figurative elements concerned. These more general strategies may involve drawing subjective, emotional, and highly personal connections, thus taking metaphor far beyond the boundaries definable by formal grammars. As Leech points out (1966:155), they may also involve reinforcements intended to signal a departure from more strictly referential speech such as alliteration, stress, or rhyme.

Although ambiguity exploits the potential of a given utterance to be derived from more than one semantic base, potential interpretations will always be limited by conventional usage. Returning to *John lives near the bank* as an illustration, the potential interpretations of the lexical item *bank* are multiple, but the probable interpretations are limited to three. The same principle of multiple, but limited, interpretation is apparent in all riddles based on formal grammatical patterns or idioms. The scope for interpretation is broadened considerably in riddles such as:

25. White bird featherless
Flew down from Paradise
Perched upon the castle wall;
Up came Lord John landless,
Took it up handless,
And rode away horseless
To the King's white hall. *Snow*.

In such riddles interpretation is guided neither by conventional grammar nor by conventional fixed usages (i.e., cliché and idiom). Matters are further complicated by the fact that such questions exist outside the realm of the conversational context (as distinct from the performance context of a riddling session). It is true that all riddles are, to a certain degree, non sequiturs. However, riddles based on ambiguity or conventional fixed usage are literal questions and, thus, susceptible to literal grammatical analysis. The present example, though based on general cognitive associations (i.e., it is derived from a relevant cultural trope), is figurative; it expresses something in terms of something else (cf. the definition of the "true riddle" in Taylor 1951). As such, riddles constructed in this manner are truly antiliteral. Perhaps a more useful term would be *a-literal*, since antiliteral would imply an inversion of fixed usage. If simple inversion were at work here, it should be possible to formulate rules of composition and solution as we have for the previously examined grammatical riddles. Happily for the creative impulse, no rules seem forthcoming. We can do little more than say their "logic" makes sense—after the fact when their answers have been revealed. Metaphorical riddles, then, seem traditional examples of what Austin 1970:24 has called in another context, "prising words off the world" or holding them apart from and against the world, so that we can realize "their inadequacies and arbitrariness," and can "re-look at the world without blinkers."

As indicated in the preceding paragraph, in regard to riddling, the act of "prising words off the world" is true not only in the larger cognitive sense, but in a more restricted one as well. Metaphorical riddles are unbounded by any conversational context that would facilitate solution. When presented with these questions, we are cut off both from universe of discourse (e.g., Is the subject biological phenomena, meteorological phenomena, behavior, or artifacts?) and mode of discourse (Is the current manner of expression literal or metaphorical?). This dilemma is roughly comparable to the situation that would obtain in nonplayful speech if we were asked, "How tall is it?" in the absence of conversational clues to delimit the referent of the pronoun *it*.

The term that best characterizes the nature of purely metaphorical riddles is *vagueness*. Ambiguity refers to the situation that exists when multiple, but limited, interpretations are possible; *vagueness* refers to situations in which the degree of description provides an inadequate basis for solution (cf. Abrahams 1968 and Abrahams and Dundes 1977, on block elements). In short, riddles utilizing linguistic ambiguity as a block element present literal questions capable of apt solution; riddles utilizing vagueness attempt to block solution by providing an inadequate cognitive basis for solution.

To this point only those vague riddles with a metaphorical base have been examined. The following riddle, although utilizing vagueness as a block, represents a different mode of operation.

26. A house full, a yard full,
    Couldn't catch a bowl full. *Smoke.*

In this case we have a question operating in the literal mode that is blocked by insufficient information to limit universe of discourse. The same strategy is manifest in riddles from which the riddlee is required to reconstruct a vignette.

27. Crooked and straight, which way are you going?
    Croptail every year, what makes you care?
    Meadow to a brook and the brook's reply.
28. Blackey went into blackey, blackey came out of blackey, and blackey left whitey in blackey.
    A black hen went into a black stump and laid a white egg.

These riddles employ metonymy (more precisely, synecdoche) and in this regard lay some claim to the techniques of figurative language, but they are clearly different in strategy from riddles utilizing intricately developed metaphorical comparisons. Metonymy is in evidence in the first of these riddles because the modifiers *crooked*, *straight*, and *croptail* are used for the referents *brook* and *meadow*. By metonymic extension the attributes of the referents are used to stand for the referents themselves. In the second example, we find clues to the answer to this riddle couched in a scheme whereby colors of the referents involved are used to signify each of the central nouns involved in the vignette.

Indeed, if we now consider both types of ambiguity just discussed, formal grammatical ambiguity and metaphorical or literary ambiguity, we discover that there are many riddles that exhibit characteristics of both types, but that fit neither category neatly. Take, for example, riddles like the following:

29. What has teeth but cannot eat? *A saw.*
30. What has a tongue and can't talk? *A shoe.*
31. Many eyes and never a nose, one tongue, and about it goes. *A shoe.*
32. What's this that's got a heart in its head? *Lettuce.*
33. There is something with a heart in its head. *A peach.*
34. What has an eye but cannot see? *A potato.*
35. Where is the smallest bridge in the world? *On your nose.*

These represent typologically inexact riddles.

In riddles 29 and 30, then, we find the metaphorical extension or comparisons of *teeth* and *tongue* are synchronically retrievable by native speakers. That is, some native speakers find the images involved still sufficiently strong to warrant calling the block element in such riddles metaphorical, although certainly not to the same degree as riddles like the elaborately metaphorical ones in 4 and 5. Indeed, the images involved must be synchronically retrievable for such riddles to be considered witty. To make this point clearer, consider for a moment riddle 31, which shares the referent *shoe* with riddle 30. Although the ambiguity of *tongue* is a factor, the elaboration of anatomical detail makes it clear that this riddle is grounded in metaphor. Riddle 30 is neither as elaborately, nor as dependently, based on metaphor as is 31.

In addition we can compare riddles 32 and 33, where the riddle questions are virtually the same, but the answers are substantially different. In 32 we see grammatical ambiguity as the major factor for creating confusion. In 33, however, there is absolutely no grammatical linguistic play, and wit relies on metaphorical language. Thus, the nondiscrete nature of the ambiguity inherent in English riddles is evidenced in these cases in two ways: (1) where the same answer is required by contrastive strategies (30 and 31); and (2) where similar questions require different strategies to discern the appropriate kind of ambiguity necessary to solve the riddle (32 and 33).

In regard to riddles 34 and 35, as we noted in our discussion of McDowell's typology, we find that the block elements have only the barest figurative connections, if any at all. Any figures contained in such riddles have either passed, or are in the process of passing, from the realm of metaphor into that of simple lexical ambiguity. This, as we also have noted, is a common occurrence in language.

At this juncture let us stop to consider what we have suggested so far. We have shown that the figurative use of ordinary language calls forth multiple frames of reference. Thus, it represents a type of ambiguity that is closely related to formal grammatical ambiguity of the type outlined in chapters 2 and 3. Also, we have demonstrated that both strategies are employed as block elements in English riddles. Despite this basic similarity, however, the two strategies differ in crucial ways. These distinct modes of operation should be distinguished, therefore, but in a way that more accurately reflects the fluid nature of language than the rigid typology posited by McDowell. For this purpose we propose a continuum with the two endpoints labeled the grammatical and the metaphorical. With such a scheme we are not bound to a static categorization; a framework of this sort is imperative. As language itself changes in respect to metaphorical usage, so that old metaphors pass into ordinary idiomatic usage, this change is reflected in the shifting of the strategies involved in riddles based on metaphorical usage along the continuum toward the formal grammatical end-point.

The following examples and their stations on our continuum illustrate the relationship we suggest in this chapter. For ease of arrangement, let us numerically tag some of the riddles discussed in this chapter.

1. In spring I am gay
   In handsome array;
   In summer more clothing I wear;
   When colder it grows
   I fling off my clothes;
   And in winter I quite naked appear. *A tree.*
2. I have a cock on yonder hill
   I keep him for a wonder
   And every time the cock do crow,
   It lightens, hails and thunders. *A gun.*
3. There is something with a heart in its head. *A peach.*
4. Blackey went into blackey, blackey came out of blackey, and blackey left whitey in blackey. *A black hen went into a black stump and laid a white egg.*
5. Crooked and straight, which way are you going?
   Croptail every year, what makes you care?
   Meadow to a brook and the brook's reply.
6. A house full, a yard full,
   Couldn't catch a bowl full. *Smoke.*
7. Many eyes and never a nose, one tongue, and about it goes. *Shoe.*
8. What has a tongue, and can't talk? *Shoe.*
9. What has teeth, but cannot eat? *Saw.*
10. What's this that's got a heart in its head? *Lettuce.*
11. Where is the smallest bridge in the world? *On your nose.*
12. What has an eye but cannot see? *A potato.*
13. What lock can no key open? *Lock of hair.*
14. What vegetable is unpopular on ships? *Leeks.*
15. How is a duck like an icicle? *Both grow down.*

16. What's black and white and red (read) all over? *Newspaper.*
17. What turns but never moves? *Milk.*

The continuum in figure 25 orders these examples according to their reliance on either metaphor or linguistic ambiguity, or some combination of the two, to create the block element(s) of each riddle. Their placements on the continuum have been determined by our analysis and have been further tested against native speaker intuition. Thirty native speakers of English with varying abilities as riddle solvers were queried as to whether each of the above examples was metaphorical or grammatical. The terms used to question informants were comparative, based on metaphor; descriptive; or literal, based on a pun, "trick" questions. Their responses vindicate our analyses. There was no difficulty in assigning the categories reflected on the continuum for riddles 1–3 and 13–17; in fact, informants unanimously agreed with our assignments (although they were not apprised of this). The more difficult riddles 4–6 were termed metaphorical by those who felt capable of labeling them at all. Predictably, our informants found examples 7–12, those at the midpoint of the continuum, more difficult to assign to categories. Our subjects often said they could be either or

Figure 25

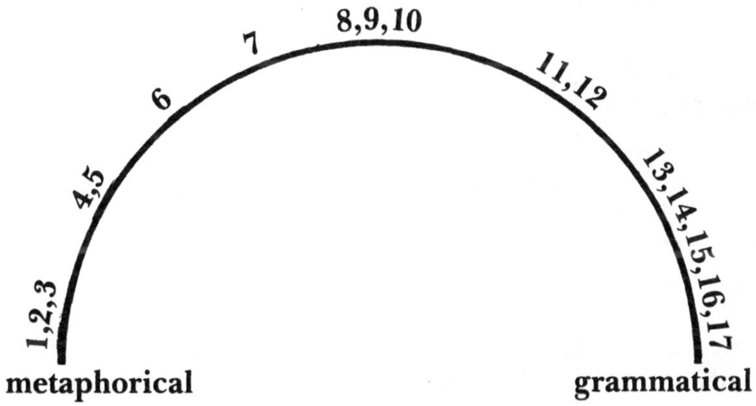

that they combined both ambiguity and metaphor. The remainder called them grammatical.

In order to characterize definite points on this continuum, let us examine each set of riddles.

Numbers 1–3 represent indisputably metaphorical riddles. In each, some quality of a specific object is compared to a similar quality of a different object. In 1, the seasonal shedding of a tree's covering is expressed in terms of a human being's disrobing. Riddle 2 compares the firing of a gun to a cock that produces lightning (the flash), hail (bullets), and thunder (the report) when it crows. (The item *cock* may also be ambiguous, since it may designate either a male fowl or the action of drawing back the hammer of a firearm.) Example 3 is built on the comparison of various physical features of a peach to anatomical structures of an animal. In this riddle, unlike the similar riddle 10, there is no opportunity for a grammatical interpretation.

Numbers 4 and 5 are not as elaborately developed as 1–3, yet, as discussed above, their reliance on metonymy as a descriptive element clearly identifies them as metaphorical.

Example 6 takes analysis into more problematic areas. Our informants frequently were unwilling to assign a label to this riddle. Those who did termed it comparative, but understandably did so intuitively without articulating their reasons for doing so. Close examination of 6 reveals that although it contains no grammatical block, it does operate in the literal mode appropriate to linguistically ambiguous riddles. Its vagueness is apparent, though. On the other hand, the direct use of metaphor that so clearly marks 1–3 as metaphorical does not appear to be in evidence in this example. Note, however, that *smoke* is placed in a frame of reference (i.e., compared) to substances that can be accumulated in bowls. Beyond vagueness, then, a descriptive device is inherent to the wit of this riddle.

The synchronically retrievable comparison of the *tongue* and *eyes* of a shoe to the *tongue* and *eyes* of an animal that coexists with the grammatical ambiguity of these lexical items gives riddle 7 qualities from both poles of our continuum. Our informants have identified this riddle either as capable of being assigned to both categories or, in a few instances, as metaphorical. This last choice, they indicate, is attributable to the elaboration of descriptive detail in this example. Such elaboration dictated our locating 7 slightly closer to the metaphorical pole than the following riddles.

Riddles 8–10 illustrate typologically inexact riddles in that, as previously noted, although the metaphorical extensions of the ambiguous terms *tongue*, *heart*, and *head* are synchronically retrievable, an equally strong case may be made for simple grammatical ambiguity. Informants were divided on the placement of these examples. The majority, though, termed them "puns."

In riddles 11 and 12, the block elements have only the barest figurative connections, if any at all. In 11, the use of *bridge* to describe the upper bony part of the nose may be claimed to be a metaphorical usage, but as such it is in need of some explanation for many native speakers. For this reason it may be claimed that the relationship between the two senses of *bridge* being employed is simple homophony rather than metaphor. Similarly, the comparison in 12 that may be claimed to render the human eye and the bud of a potato as being similar is weaker than the images in 8–10. That is, historically *eye* meaning *bud* is a metaphorical extension, but synchronically, in the active grammar of a current native speaker who does not have access to the history of the individual words of the language, this figurative connection may be either weak or nonexistent. This figure, then, either has passed, or is in the process of passing from the realm of metaphor to that of simple lexical ambiguity. Informants almost unanimously called these examples puns, although a few did see some underlying metaphorical qualities in the block.

The final segment of the continuum, 13–17, contains those riddles that, according to our analyses and informants' interpretations, contain strictly grammatical blocks.

By means of this analysis, we discover that ambiguity constitutes a useful means for explicating the block elements in riddles in the English language. Unlike the rigid categories proposed in previous works, however, the use of a continuum more accurately reflects the relationships between grammatical and metaphorical riddles found in our corpus. We find, also, that the categories are fairly stable in structure only at the extremes of our spectrum. Between these extremes we find examples that fit neither category exactly but that exhibit qualities of both. By identifying various points along this continuum, we hope to have facilitated understanding of the ranges of ambiguous utterance and the ways in which both metaphorical and grammatical ambiguity are manipulated to create wit in riddling and other genres of verbal art.

Let us now consider our continuum of ambiguity and the metaphor paradigm in a more inclusive linguistic context, namely that of semiotics. In this way we can relate the formalizable elements of wit and the conventions dictating its use and interpretation to the overall system of human communication. We have already discussed the nature of linguistic sign in our discussion of metaphor. All language, of course, including metaphor, is representative. That is, it is composed of signs that refer to something else. In metaphor this is perhaps most clear. But the same semiotic analysis holds for the grammatically ambiguous language we have been discussing. For example, in the riddle "What turns but never moves? Milk" *turns* is a sign that has more than one possible referent. The same is true for the sequence *grow down* in the riddle "Why is a duck like an icicle? Both grow down." Thus, from a semiotic viewpoint, the continuum of ambiguity we have outlined can be treated as a whole in that it deals with the relationship of signans to signatum.

We find, however, that there is a basic difference in the nature of this relationship in metaphorical ambiguity as opposed to grammatical ambiguity. Specifically, metaphor functions in a paradigmatic mode, grammatical ambiguity functions in a syntagmatic mode. That is, metaphor functions according to systematized similarity that is focused upon by means of comparison, but grammatical ambiguity functions by contiguity, i.e., by its context. Thus, metaphorical riddles are solvable by resource to the appropriate paradigm, although riddles based on grammatical ambiguity must be linguistically contextualized (i.e., placed into a discourse) to be solvable. This is not to say that context plays no part in metaphorical riddles, but rather to point out that metaphorical paradigms are the basic strategy in such riddles.

Between these two extremes we have riddles that function by a combination of paradigmatic and syntagmatic strategies, for example, our riddles 26–28:

26. A house full, a yard full,
    Couldn't catch a bowl full. *Smoke.*
27. Crooked and straight, where are you going?
    Croptail every year, what makes you care?
    Meadow to a brook and the brook's reply.
28. Blackey went into blackey, blackey came out of blackey, and blackey left whitey in blackey. *A black hen went into a black stump and laid a white egg.*

In these riddles we find that imagery is a basic strategy, but that the image itself acts by contiguity. That is, since the image is not direct (metonymy, rather than metaphor proper, is employed), it is dependent upon its context for clarity. In riddling, of course, context is suspended, and so the overt comparisons of such riddles are submerged. The riddlee resorts to shared cultural knowledge and/or immediate linguistic context (the riddle unit) in his attempt to solve the riddles.

Such a strategy for solution is complicated by the nature of linguistic sign. For, as pointed out by the Prague School linguists, the sign and its meaning do not cover, in all their points, the same field (see Vachek 1970:31). Specifically, one sign may have several functions. This is the case with the verb *turn* discussed above, and is a basic ploy of riddles that use grammatical ambiguity, or homophony. On the other hand, one and the same meaning can be expressed by several signs, i.e., signs may be synonymous. As pointed out by Karchevsky 1929, each linguistic sign is homonymous and synonymous at the same time and is constituted by the mutual crossing of those two series of considered facts. He represents this relationship as in figure 26. The

Figure 26

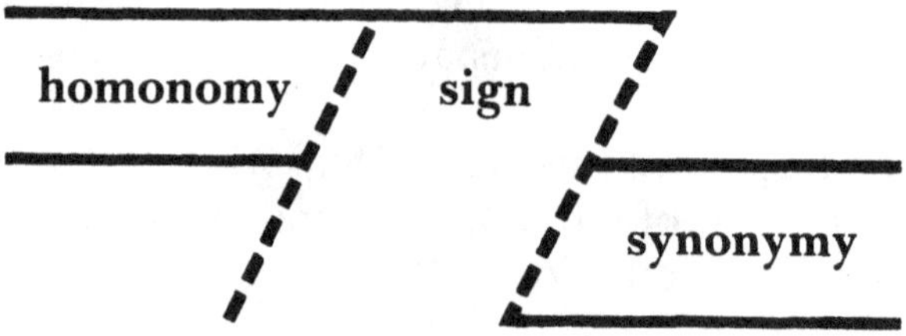

relationship of signans to signatum, then, is a sliding one. A sign has functions other than the one found in a particular context; content can be expressed by other than a primary sign in any context. We thus have an asymmetrical relationship that shifts according to context. Riddles, then, manipulate the pivotal semiotic element, context, in creating confusion.

Jakobson 1971 deals with the notions of similarity versus contiguity in his treatment of the differences between metaphor and metonymy. He sees metaphor and metonymy as polar types of figures in that one topic leads to another through similarity in the case of metaphor, and through contiguity in the case of metonymy. We have suggested that grammatical ambiguity depends even more on contiguity than metonymy does, since no "topic" or image is involved, so that grammatical ambiguity is solvable only by recourse to connected discourse. In any event, the point here is that the signans-signatum relationship depends on context, and riddles suspend all normal context. Thus the linguistic sign is not interpretable within a definable locus. One task of the riddlee is to try to place the sign, whatever its nature, in a locus that permits a definition of the signans-signatum relationship, and that permits a definition of the signans-signatum relationship, and thus a solution to the riddle. This task is complicated further in that riddles may employ both metaphor and metonymy, i.e., the strategies of similarity and contiguity in combination, to confuse the riddlee.

Let us consider two examples in more detail:

36. White comes out of white, and run white out of white. *A white dog runs out of a white house and chases a white cow out of a cotton patch.*
37. Two legs sat on three legs.
    Up jumped four legs
    And grabs one leg.
    Man sitting on a three-legged stool; up jump a dog and grabs ham on the table.

As in cases of metonymy, such as "five sails" signifying "five ships" or the reference to the range of physical sustenance as "daily bread," riddles 36 and 37 employ one element of an entity to refer to the whole. Though both 36 and 37 utilize the artistic device of metonymy, 37 adds an additional twist. In 36 we have a literal, though vague in the sense of the term we have introduced, riddle utilizing only metonymy as a block element. The single element "whiteness" is used to refer to a variety of phenomena that share this attribute of color despite the drastic differences among these phenomena when perceived in their entirety. In 37, however, we note that the riddle employs not only metonymy—the parts "legs" (specifically the respective number of legs) as signifiers of the things to which these limbs are attached—but a certain degree of linguistic ambiguity is also apparent. That is, on the lexical level, *legs* may designate both the appendages used to support living creatures and the structural supports of furniture. As a result the solution of the riddle requires one to perceive both metonymy and the ambiguity of the signans.

It is thus observed that metonymy in riddles is of a different order than other manifestations of the trope. The differences noted result from the fact that in other usages the referent of the metonym is rendered immediately and manifestly clear by contextual markers, so that context reveals the paradigmatic aspects of the figure. In the case of riddles, even the most literal, the image is denied a disambiguating context. Moreover, many of the riddles we have designated as formally ambiguous (because that is the *primary* device for generating the block element) also owe some of their force to metonymy, since one attribute is selected from the bundle of attributes comprising the particular entity signified. Such selection is based on the fact that the name of the characteristic chosen lends itself to the creation of linguistic ambiguity. The following riddles illustrate this argument.

38. What has an eye but cannot see? *Needle.*

39. What has a mouth but does not eat? *River.*

40. What has teeth but does not eat? *Comb.*

Although riddles 38–40 are best classified as examples of linguistic ambiguity at the lexical level, at some intermediate stage between the perception of the referent and its description in the riddling context, selection of a representative attribute—metonymy—has taken place.

These last riddles are to be distinguished from riddles like "What turns but never moves? Milk" where the strategy is purely grammatical. In examples 26–28 and 36–37, the riddlee is presented only partial descriptions; often these descriptions select only a single aspect of the referent and modify this aspect in some fashion. Clearly, then, the principle of metonymy is integral to the process of riddling.

It should be noted here that the signans-signatum relationships we have outlined follow our continuum of ambiguity from the literary to the grammatical, with transitional types between the two extremes. That is, we find strict paradigmatic relationships between signans and signatum in riddles like 4 and 5 earlier in the chapter. We find strict syntagmatic relationships in riddles like 1–3. Finally, in riddles like those just discussed, we find both relationships employed in the creation of block elements.

1. See Lyons 1969, Nida 1948, and Plato, *Kratylos.*

COMMUNICATIVE STRUCTURE IN RIDDLES

Chapter Seven

THE RELATIONSHIP BETWEEN formal ambiguity and less literal, metaphorical ambiguity as techniques for riddle confusion has been demonstrated by our riddle continuum and our accompanying discussion. In light of the previous observation that the nature of art is representative and thus comparative, we might now ask whether other traditional forms may be found that draw their vitality from the principles described earlier. An examination of proverbs provides a useful point of departure. Although a systematic presentation does not exist, relationships between riddle and proverb have not gone unnoticed. On the most superficial level, folklorists have labelled both forms "minor genres." The term *minor* undoubtedly connoted, at one stage in the development of folkloristics, "less interesting" or "of peripheral concern," especially when compared to the major genres such as folktale or folksong. Certainly when folklore was a discipline devoted to the examination of oral literature, folk narrative and lyric provided more fertile fields to till. Now, however, most folklorists would disavow this pejorative sense of the term *minor*. Minor at this point may aptly refer to textual brevity, and in this sense, proverb and riddle are minor. They are among the briefest forms of utterance in the traditional repertoire that utilize the techniques of art as framing devices. That is, both genres are "witty" in the restricted sense that we have employed in this study.

On the other hand, proverb and riddle characteristically are placed in opposition by virtue of the goals of their respective performances. Proverbs seek to reduce confusion through the artful relocation of a real social problem; riddles seek to create fictitious problems, competitive events that intensify social disparity. Let us briefly clarify this point. The proverb in a situation of social conflict is introduced as a device for managing the confusion created therein. It does so, as Burke 1941 has pointed out, by means of classifying the distinct situation into a general category and proposing a strategy for resolving it. Thus, tension arises before the performance event, is addressed through artful means, and is confronted upon the return of the audience (the recipient of the advice) to social reality. The goal of this performance, therefore, is the reintroduction of stasis in the audience.

Thus proverbs seek to enhance sociability. After all, they exist to present to their troubled recipients courses of action that tradition has shown to be apt solutions to recurrent social problems. In order to encourage the acceptance of the advice rendered, our cultural tradition, and apparently most others, have built into proverbs a variety of devices designed to dispell any impressions of individual authoritarianism or direct criticism. Of course, relegating one's particular problem to a general class of recurrent situations signals that this situation is not due to an individual peculiarity, but is widely spread in the given culture. Framing the proffered advice by introducing it with the phrase, "You know what they say," marks the advice as traditional wisdom, thus negating this advice as a personal attack. Proverbs, in fact, seem to employ a number of relocation devices (cf. Abrahams 1972). Certainly metaphor is one of these devices, since it deals with a social situation only by analogy to an imaginary world. In addition, we find that in proverbs the use of abstraction is frequent, as in "Necessity is the mother of invention." We also find the use either of third-person pronouns, as in "He who hesitates is lost," or the use of the "impersonal you," as in "You can't get blood out of a turnip." All of these devices serve to underplay features of difference by means of both linguistic and sociolinguistic mechanisms.

Riddling performances, conversely, are competitive, rather than cooperative, enterprises. Rather than working with the audience to restore proper (i.e., socially functional) perception of a situation, the riddler foists confusion on his audience by a variety of means. Despite the resolution of conflict with the supplying of the answer, riddles seek to generate tension as consciously as proverbs try to ameliorate it. This is true of the social strategies of riddling, as well as of the linguistic strategies we have discussed. In riddling we are allowed, even required, to be rude. There is disparity between the interactants; riddlers are the final arbiters of the answers provided by riddlees. Moreover, outside this particular performance context their judgments would generally be condemned as being excessively capricious. In addition, the norms of expectation for interrogation are inverted in riddle sessions. In nonplayful speech one only imposes questions upon parties he believes capable of providing answers. In riddling, however, the riddler only presents those questions for which he believes riddlees cannot provide answers. Finally, in riddling any textual or contextual clues that might be forthcoming in ordinary talk are submerged and obscured as far as is allowable within the prevailing performance tradition. In essence, riddling thrives on rending the social and communicative bonds between participants.

Though the goals of the performances thus constitute polarities, the means to their respective ends do not. We have established the metaphorical nature of many riddles. Similarly, Abrahams (1976:199) states, "The proverb-sayer appeals, directly or by analogy, to an approved course of action." Even more explicit is the argument in Seitel 1976:129 that an "Important aspect of proverb use . . . is the metaphorical relationship between the situation presented literally in the proverb and the context situation to which the proverb refers." Given these similarities, a systematization of the relationships between these forms and their common base, metaphor, should be possible.

Barthes 1964 provides us with a point of departure in his assertion that aphoristic types of discourse are of the metaphoric order. If this is the case, the interrelationships of metaphor, proverb, and at least a large body of riddles should be demonstrable. To begin, the similarity in structure of the three forms may be arranged paradigmatically in terms of standard semiotic analysis by their correlation to the terms *sign*, *signifier*, and *signified*. *Sign* designates "the mark of an intention to communicate a meaning" (see Guiraud, 1971:23). All signs are comprised of a signifier (that which refers to or stands for another concept) and the signified (the concept communicated by the signifier). The nature of metaphor, proverb, and riddle as signs can thus be rendered as in figure 27.

With pure metaphor the signifier-signified relation is straightforward, and this relationship is the basis of the paradigm. In the case of proverb, the relationship is also fairly clear and has been outlined by Seitel 1976 in his work, as we have noted. Specifically, Seitel schematizes proverb in terms of "metaphorical reasoning," whereby an imaginary (proverb) situation is applied to a real situation through a process of correlation. This view is supported by Burke 1973.

Figure 27

Sign	Signifier	Signified
Metaphor	Figure	Object, Phenomenon
Riddle	Question-Answer Unit	Mastery of linguistic code
Proverb	Statement	Strategy

For the riddle, however, the situation is somewhat different. The signifier in the case of riddles is the question-answer unit that characterizes the riddle act. We have seen in the last chapter that the signified of riddles is not readily defined, and indeed we will need to distinguish several signata, according to our own analysis. Let us first address the question of why the signified of the riddle is not simply "the answer." Indeed, in some cases this would seem to be true, especially for metaphorically-based riddles. For instance, in the riddle "What's that got its heart in its head? A peach," one might assume a simple relationship parallel to that for metaphor obtains in the riddle structure. There are many instances, however, in which this cannot be true. For example, many riddles are not framed as questions, e.g., numbers 4 and 5 in chapter 6. Such riddles certainly have the illocutionary force of questions, but the signifier is unrecognizable as such outside of a riddling context. Thus it is inappropriate to treat the poem as a signifier and the referent as a signified; the riddle must be treated as a unit to be intelligible.

This argument is strengthened when we consider riddles based on formal grammatical ambiguity. Such riddles clearly do not have a "referent" as a signified. In a riddle question like "Why is coffee like the soil? It is ground," we have evidence for this in two respects. First, the solution to this riddle lies in the grammar of English and depends upon a resolution of morphological ambiguity in the phonological sequence /grawnd/. Second, and more important, the ambiguity on which this riddle turns is found *in the answer*. Thus the answer is not "a solution" as such; it is rather part of a question-answer sequence that focuses on the pliability of the linguistic code in English. The same is true for examples like "How is a duck like an icicle? Both grow down."

What we need, then, is a relationship of signifier to signified that will encompass both metaphorical riddles and those based on grammatical ambiguity, providing a statement of the signified of the riddle form in general terms. In the case of riddles based on grammatical ambiguity, the signified seems to be the pliability of the linguistic code. That is, such riddles focus on aspects of formal grammar that may be manipulated for ludic effect. Thus the signified in such riddles is twofold. First, it is the pliability of the grammar itself. Second, it is the actual manipulation, i.e., the riddle act. The same is true in large part for metaphorically-based riddles. Here the twofold nature of the signified is as follows: As we have pointed out, these riddles are concerned with a manipulation of the formal linguistic code. The second aspect of metaphorically-based riddles is, again as with grammatically-based ones, concerned with the riddle act itself, but is more complex in that the manipulation involves the figures of speech we have outlined.

We see, then, that the signified of these two types of riddles are similar. What remains is to distill its essence, if possible. Perhaps as close as we can come to this goal is to point out that the signified of riddles is not an object or situation, but rather the code itself. This means that riddles are metalinguistic, i.e., they are a way of using language to deal with language. In this case "deal with" means "exhibit mastery of." This metalinguistic view of riddles accounts for the fact that all riddles are highly decontextualized. In order to talk about language, we must first suspend all linguistic context, so that we do not confuse the language we are talking about with the language we are using to talk about it. As we have pointed out, riddles depend upon such suspension of linguistic context. We might mention further that this same suspension of context acts in the social mode to allow reversal of normal power structures, so that in a riddling session it is the riddler who is in authority, whatever his status outside of a session is vis à vis other members of that session.

In an effort to explicate the paradigmatic nature of metaphor, it is useful to characterize the notion of metaphorical description as "variations on a theme." Despite the difficulties presented by describing metaphor by metaphorical means, this allows us to perceive what happens when we move from denotation to connotation. For example, the term *life* has been variously described as "a tale told by an idiot," "a game of chess," and "a card game." Though the emphases are clearly different in the various figures of speech—meaninglessness, strategic challenge, and the interplay of determinism and free will—these topics all contribute to and are enhanced by a single world-view. Thus, we might say that these, and in fact all our metaphors referring to life, constitute a paradigm. Though he made these comments about a single figure of speech, the argument of J. I. Levin that "the poetic attitude toward the world is characterized by the aspiration to seize the perceived object simultaneously from different sides, to catch *in a single act* of perception and description the varied bonds and relations in which this object functions" (1977:203) accurately describes the nature of such metaphor paradigms.

Riddles, too, constitute paradigms of perception for their referents. Metaphorical riddles referring to *man* may be used as examples.

1. It first walks on four legs, then on two, then on three legs. *Man.*
2. What tree grows without roots? *Human being.*
3. The tree has only two leaves, what is it? *A man and his ears.*

In riddles 1, 2, and 3 we see a descriptive paradigm that we may label *man*. Though different qualities are called forth in each case, all contribute to the group's understanding of what it means to be human. These riddle metaphors differ from nonenigmatic figures in that they adhere to what J. I. Levin has called the "riddle principle," that is, "the principle of deliberately impeded form" that furthers "extricating the thing from the automatism of perception" (1977:203). Ben-Amos (1976:251) emphasizes the automaticity of the bonds and relations in paradigmatic riddle metaphor in his discussion of culture-specific limits on such paradigms. Thus, it might be argued that by deliberately blocking perception (i.e., solution), group members are forced to come to terms with the qualities of humanness that are rehearsed in their traditional verbal arts.

Proverbs, as noted above, classify individual dilemmas into categories of recurrent social problems. Though these problems are of a general nature, and thus each paradigm must be labelled according to the major maladjustment the proverbs within it seek to redress, each flaw in the social fabric is mended by a slightly different proverbial stitch. Let us take as our examples: "Strike while the iron is hot"; "He who hesitates is lost"; and "A stitch in time saves nine." Each of these bits of traditional advice has a slightly different orientation, but it is clear that each is intended to address the problems brought on by delaying appropriate action. In terms of interrelationships between verbal art and social conditions, inappropriate behavior serves as a catalyst; the proverb characterizes this behavior figuratively, and the strategy for solving the given problem may be regarded as its referent. Therefore, we have a similar pattern at work as described for the two preceding forms. This similarity may be represented as in figure 28.

Figure 28

	Metaphor	**Riddle**	**Proverb**
Referent	**Life**	**Man**	**Problem caused by delaying action**
Figure/ Trope	**1) tale told by an idiot** **2) game of chess** **3) card game**	**1) 4 legs, 2 legs, then 3 legs** **2) What (tree) grows without roots?** **3) the tree has only 2 leaves, what is it?**	**1) Strike while the iron is hot.** **2) He who hesitates is lost.** **3) A stitch in time, saves nine.** **4) Pull and Pray**

In the light of such similarities, we are forced to conclude that differences in these forms lie not in the texts themselves, but in the contexts in which the respective forms are embedded. Let us consider the respective contexts, then, and examine how context plays a major role in the production and interpretation of these forms in their proper use.

In our discussion of the continuum of ambiguity from the formal grammatical type to the metaphorical type, it should be apparent that the definition of ambiguity is much more precise in the former case than in the latter. Thus, as we move away from grammatically-based blocks in riddles, we find that the terms "vagueness" and "metaphorical ambiguity" are characterized as more generally cognitive notions, and thus are less amenable to formal analysis. In view of recent works on metaphor, and of our own discussion, it is possible to discuss some of the strategies involved in our comprehension and appreciation of metaphor in riddles as well as in other genres.

In several recent works from the fields of folklore, semiotics, and linguistics, authors have been concerned with the interpretation that we give to innovative use in language. An examination of three representative works spanning these fields reveals a common focus of concern, namely, the role of context in determining an interpretation of innovative uses of language. By context we designate a number of factors affecting interpretation, including at least surrounding spoken or written material, real-world physical setting, and the social situation involved in the use of innovative language.

Beginning with the narrowest contextual focus, let us consider the work of J. I. Levin 1977. Levin treats metaphor as a figure that "seizes a perceived object simultaneously from different sides," that catches "in a single act of perception and description the varied bonds and relations in which this object functions" (1977:203). He describes two principles involved in the metaphorical process, the principle of comparison and the riddle principle. The former is used to categorize types of metaphor; the latter is invoked to characterize metaphor as a "deliberately impeded form" that furthers "extricating the thing from the automatism of perception" (1977:203).

Levin's principles and categories are reminiscent of many previous works that deal with the metaphorical base of riddles, especially the work of Taylor 1951 and more recently the works of Hamnett 1967 and Glazier and Glazier 1976. His contribution to this tradition lies in his attempt to categorize the structure of metaphor according to contextual properties. Simply put, Levin claims that in any given context there are words that are "normal," i.e., acceptable, in that context. For example, in the context [I love the — — — of forests] the blank may be filled by such words as *smell* or *freshness*. Such words are said to be "marked" for this context. On the other hand, there are words that may appear in a context that are not marked for that context, e.g., *whispers* in the above context. It is precisely when a word (or phrase) that is not marked for a given context appears in that context that metaphorical convention is invoked.

Using the formalization of formal logic, Levin describes several types of situations that require metaphorical interpretation. Such situations include: (1) those where a word is "accentuated and acquires more weight than that attributed by the vocabulary" or (2) a word is joined to another word with which it is not normally associated (e.g., *a cheerful lamp*). Levin presents other categories, but although his formalism of contextual considerations is unique, it suffers two basic drawbacks. First, the underlying notions of markedness and contextuality that he uses are merely revivals of Prague School theory which is well-known. More important, his formalism, although it provides a focus for his work, does not advance our understanding of how metaphor works; it merely affords yet another classification of form involving a rudimentary semantic theory that is internal to his system.

In a work dealing with metaphor in proverbs, Seitel 1976 focuses on the broader contextual aspects of metaphor in that genre. Drawing on the works of Firth 1926 and Arewa and Dundes 1964, he rightly points out that the metaphor of proverbs must be considered in light of the situations that dictate its use, effect, restrictions, and significance in speech. Of primary importance for Seitel is the determination of the interaction of culturally defined features in a specific context (which he terms the "interaction situation"). His framework for interpretation of metaphor involves such factors as the relationship of the speaker to the hearer (e.g., age, sex) and the aptness of the analogy between the imaginary world of metaphor (the proverb) and the real, social situation to which the metaphor is applied.

Of importance for our present discussion is Seitel's description of the proverb (or the metaphor of the proverb) from which he draws the framework for interpretation we have just outlined. He characterizes this use of metaphor as short, traditional, and "out of context." By "out of context" he means that metaphors, especially proverbial ones, may be inappropriate to a conversation by virtue of syntax or, more commonly, subject matter. Thus, to use the phrase "A stitch in time saves nine" to refer to having one's car serviced at regular intervals may seem inappropriate, but this use is in fact acceptable and sanctioned within the context of a specific conversation.

Seitel goes on to point out that within the context of a given situation, various elements of a metaphor may be foregrounded, emphasized or literalized. Thus, the phrase "Don't send a boy to do a man's job" may be used appropriately in a situation where a child has been asked to perform a task of which he is incapable, in which case the image is applied correctly and literally; metaphor is not invoked. Here the actual physical situation is foregrounded. On the other hand, the same phrase may be used to characterize a situation wherein a person has been assigned a task for which he is incompetent. In this case it is the impotence of a person in a given situation that is focused upon.

Seitel's work does much to advance our understanding of how we interpret metaphor in the proverb. His work also provides us with an insight into the workings of metaphor in riddles. For both Seitel and Levin, context is a central factor in the interpretation of metaphor. As emphasized by Levin, context must include a wide range of social considerations.

It is this factor of context that is crucial to the use of metaphor in riddling. As we have pointed out, riddling suspends elements of context in order to intensify certain aspects of the linguistic code of language. Riddling sessions depend upon a willing suspension of utilitarian context on the part of the participants in favor of a ludic alternative. Grammatical ambiguity, as we have noted, is difficult to perceive, and thus to resolve, if there is no discourse to provide clues for disambiguation. The same is true for the use of metaphor in riddles. Riddling suspends not only linguistic context, but the serious elements of social context as well. The roles of riddler and riddlee are defined, but the rules of normal conversation are suspended, thus eliminating any contextualization of the riddle metaphor within a conventional, utilitarian locus.

Thus, one may recognize that a given riddle is employing a metaphor as its block element but be unable to solve the riddle. Metaphors arise from negotiations *between* cognitive frameworks; therefore there is no unequivocable framework within which to place the metaphor in order to interpret it. Further, without a specifiable context, it is in principle impossible to determine which aspects of a riddle metaphor are being foregrounded and are therefore most relevant for solving the riddle.

Yet clearly riddles, whether based on grammatical or metaphorical ambiguity, or on one of the transitional types we have described, are solvable within the confines of a culture. There are strategies, such as those we have noted in our analysis of grammatically-based riddles, that facilitate the perception and resolution of ambiguity in the riddle. For grammatically ambiguous riddles these strategies are fairly well-defined. In the case of metaphorically-based riddles, however, the strategies are more diverse and include a wide range of cognitive concerns, as we have seen. This does not mean that metaphorical riddles defy all attempts at a formalization of their mechanisms of wit, however. For if we again approach metaphor from a linguistic point of view, we find that recent developments in linguistic analyses of innovative language use afford insights into the interpretation of metaphor, and thus into the use of metaphor in riddles.

In a recent article in *Language*, Eve and Herbert Clark discuss the kinds of strategies involved in the use and interpretation of denominal verbs (Clark and Clark 1979). Denominal verbs denote those verbs that originate from the use of a noun to denote action associated with that noun, for example *John Houdini'd the lock open*, or *He wristed the ball over the net*. Their concern in this article is to define how the use of such verbs is regulated by convention, and how such verbs are able to be interpreted on a particular occasion. Let us now examine some of their arguments and conclusions and consider the relevance of their findings to our study of metaphor and riddles.

The Clarks claim that innovative denominal verbs function by a shifting denotation. That is, every word normally has a fixed denotation or denotations of the type listed in dictionaries. Thus a word like *bachelor*, to use an example made famous by Katz and Fodor 1963, has four denotations: (1) 'an unmarried man,' (2) 'young knight,' (3) 'person with a baccalaureate degree,' and (4) 'mateless breeding fur seal.' Normally the number of denotations is fairly small, but it is at least finite for all words.

This type of fixed denotational expression is distinct from what are called indexical or deictic expressions, which have a fixed denotation but a shifting reference. Thus the pronoun *she* has a fixed meaning of 'female person,' but the specific person to whom it refers—its referent—changes according to contextual features such as we have discussed. In this same way, although *bachelor* is purely denotational, *the bachelor* is indexical in that its referent may change from one use to the next.

The Clarks argue that denominal verbs form yet a third category, which they label "contextuals." They claim that contextual expressions have a shifting denotation, and that the denotation of such expressions is dependent upon context. They propose three criteria for the definition of a contextual. The first is that the possible number of denotations is indefinitely large. This criterion is inextricably linked with the second one, which is that the denotation depends upon context. Since the possible contexts for the use of a contextual are indefinitely many, so are the denotations, or possible interpretations, of a contextual. The final criterion is one of cooperation between speaker and listener. That is, the use of contextuals demands that the listener take note of the specific context, including such things as previous references, idiosyncratic allusions, unique gestures, and other "momentary relevant facts about the conversation."

Another crucial factor in the use of contextuals, according to the Clarks, is the exploitation of mutual knowledge. They distinguish two types of knowledge in the world, the generic and the particular. The generic encompasses those things that it can be assumed are known by most people. The particular includes those things that people know tacitly and depends crucially upon the individual histories of people. The particular includes esoteric or idiosyncratic information, or even misinformation about the world. They claim that contextuals depend primarily on generic knowledge, and that it is this fact that makes innovative uses of language, like contextuals, interpretable.

Let us pause now to consider what has just been outlined in light of what has been said about metaphor, riddling, and proverb. It should be clear that metaphorical language falls into the category of contextuals. That is, metaphor takes an expression with a literal denotation and, by virtue of context in its broadest sense, foregrounds one or more elements of that expression so that the expression receives a unique interpretation according to context. Thus metaphor involves a shifting denotation of an expression, as determined by context, within the limits of cultural convention. Further, metaphor is crucially dependent upon mutual knowledge, which includes at the most general level a sharing of cultural conventions, all the way to shared knowledge of a fairly idiosyncratic type. One of the limiting forces on metaphor is mutual knowledge, since speaker and hearer must share enough knowledge to enable the listener to discern which features of a metaphorical expression are salient in a given context. Indeed, a lack of shared knowledge results in metaphors that are meaningless to listeners, and thus relegated to the ill-defined category of nonmetaphors, i.e., attempts at metaphor that fail for some reason.

Thus the Clarks provide a partial definition of the metaphorical trope through their characterization of contextuals, and in so doing also provide some insight into some of the cultural limitations places on what is, and what is not, a metaphor in a culture. But given their criteria for contextuals, we might still seek a set of principles or strategies for interpreting these innovative uses of language. They offer such a strategy by claiming that in using innovative denominal verbs, "a speaker means to denote:

(a) a kind of situation
(b) that he has good reason to believe
(c) that on this occasion the listener can readily compute
(d) uniquely
(e) on the basis of their mutual knowledge
(f) in such a way that the parent noun denotes one role in the state, event or process, and the remaining surface arguments of the denominal verb denote others of its roles." (1979:787)

This strategy, they claim, allows a speaker to interpret an innovative use of a contextual on a particular occasion. We have already dealt with most of the elements of this strategy, but we will now comment at more length on the individual components.

Elements (a)–(e) all deal with the context of an innovative use. Element (a) is focused upon separately in that the situation being denoted has certain cultural features associated with it that determine which elements of the situation are likely to be foregrounded and thus are more susceptible to innovative use. The Clarks use the example of the phase "porch the paper" where our knowledge of the basic relationships between porches and papers allows us to interpret the usage of "porch" as meaning "placed on the porch," rather than, for example, "placed under the porch," under normal circumstances. The element of situation is certainly crucial to our interpretation of metaphor, also since our cultural knowledge of the salient features of any situation, say cooking a meal, will determine what aspects of the situation are likely to be focussed upon in innovative metaphorical usage and how the resultant figurative usage will be interpreted.

Elements (b) and (c) are concerned with speaker-listener cooperation. First, the speaker must use innovative language in good faith, i.e., in the belief that his innovation is interpretable. Second, he must construct his innovative use of language so that the listener is capable of interpreting the innovation based on stored shared knowledge. The implications for metaphorical usage should be clear in this instance. We must assume that the user of metaphor has a reason for using it and that he has facilitated our understanding of his particular innovative construction by providing us adequate means for interpretation.

Passing over element (e) for the moment, element (f) provides a strategy for interpreting the action indicated by an innovative denominal verb. It assumes that we view a verb as being composed of a proposition or action and a number of arguments, i.e., persons or objects that are involved in or related to the proposition in some specifiable way. Thus a sentence like *Abe gave Mary a pencil* contains a proposition *give* and the arguments *Abe* (subject), *Mary* (indirect object), and *pencil* (direct object). In the case of denominal verbs, one argument must be the noun from which the verb is derived (the parent noun). Thus, for *He wristed the ball over the net*, one argument of the verb *wrist* is the noun *wrist*, which is an instrumental argument indicating manner.

This specific strategy is applicable to metaphor in that the propositions and roles of metaphorical expression must involve a set of relationships that are analogous to a real situation in a recognizable way, thus rendering the comparison of the two frames of reference acceptable. There must be at least a partial one-to-one correspondence between the arguments and/or propositions in the situations being compared, so that the listener can make the appropriate substitutions of arguments and propositions necessary for interpretation of the innovative usage.

Let us now return to element (e), that of uniqueness of interpretation. This element is at once the most interesting and the most elusive. Although unique interpretation is often a goal in the use of denominal verbs, as well as of metaphor, it is in principle impossible to attain. In the case of denominal verbs, unique interpretation is perhaps attainable if the speaker of an innovative verb and his listener have a complete shared knowledge. However, any differences in knowledge between the two, however subtle the nuance, may result in a nonunique interpretation, i.e., an instance in which the message encoded by the speaker is not the same as the one decoded by the listener. To some extent, context will serve to preserve uniqueness of interpretation, but even here, speaker and hearer may have different perspectives.

From the point of view of metaphor, uniqueness of interpretation is a well-known problem. The interpretation of a figure of speech, though grounded in generic knowledge, is notoriously susceptible to the highly personal, emotional, and idiosyncratic nuances that result from individual differences in listeners. Indeed, part of the "experience of literature" is the bringing of particular knowledge (as discussed above) to the work being read (or heard). Since the individual histories of listeners or readers may vary, the particular knowledge that each person employs in interpreting a given image will vary in unpredictable ways. In this way "personal interpretation" is allowed for and literary debate engendered.

Let us expand this last point, since it seems reasonable to ask how metaphor can be a base for genres like the riddle or proverb if it is subject to personalization. In the case of riddles, there is much less appeal to the level of particular knowledge, since metaphorical riddles are framed in such a way as to induce the riddlee to draw on his generic knowledge to recognize the referent being described. Highly idiosyncratic riddles (excluding neck riddles) are generally unacceptable. The performance context of riddles dictates that the imagery of metaphorical riddles be accessible to anyone who enters the riddling session, and so naturally leads the participants to operate at a generic knowledge level.

The case with proverbs is somewhat different, however, A proverb draws its force not from a performance context as such, but rather from a specific social situation in which it is invoked. Thus one proverb may be applied to a number of different specific situations (or vice versa). Whereas the riddle metaphor depends upon lack of social context for its effect, the proverb metaphor is highly contextualized, and the foregrounded elements of the metaphor are in part determined by the immediate context. As Kenneth Burke 1941:293 has noted, proverbs "name typical, recurrent situations" within a given society. Although each group has a traditional set of recurrent problems that may be addressed by a specific set of standardized strategies (Burke identifies consolation, vengeance, admonition, exhortation, and foretelling, for example), any set of formulae must be finite. The situations causing social friction, on the other hand, are infinite. Therefore, flexibility must be built into any classificatory system if it is to prove useful over the long haul. We shall address this flexibility in detail in a moment.

Burke indicates his recognition of this principle in his discussion of the proverb "Virtue flies from the heart of a mercenary man." This maxim, he writes, may have a range of applications: "A poor man might obviously use it either to console himself for being poor (the implication being, 'Because I am poor in money I am rich in virtue') or to strike at another (the implication being 'When he got money, what else could you expect of him but deterioration?'). In fact, we could even say that such symbolic vengeance would itself be an aspect of solace" (1941:296). What Burke does not deal with, however, are those factors in the proverb text and context that allow its application to this broad range of social problems.

A general strategy in this regard is suggested by Archer Taylor in his observation that "proverbs develop from the generalization of a simple scene" (1931:142). Rather than adhering to Taylor's developmental argument, we shall be content to assert that proverbs draw rhetorical force from the fact that they allow for generalization based upon the image of a simple scene. In other words, a common general truth unites both a particular problematic situation and an imaginary situation that serves to name, i.e., categorize, the real situation.

By way of pursuing this point, consider the proverb "A rolling stone gathers no moss." The basic metaphor, one of change and the resulting absence of permanence, is clear. However, without a context it is impossible to determine whether the statement is positive, e.g., lauding the virtues of independence generated by adaptability to current situations, or negative, e.g., a condemnation of "rootlessness." Only in a specific context can we determine which aspects of the figure are being emphasized (see Dundes 1975). In this way proverb metaphor is clearly a contextual, in the sense used of denominal verbs. However, with proverb metaphor we see a much greater influence of particular knowledge, since the use of a proverb is provoked by an individual's reaction to a specific situation, and this reaction is in large part dictated by the individual's personal history. The proverb metaphor employed by a given person in a given situation, then, allows that person to categorize the situation in a way consistent with his own cognitive framework for dealing with the world. Such subjectification of situations leads naturally to conflicts between persons, since their particular knowledges may have points of difference, or gaps, vis à vis one another. Thus it is that one person may not understand another's use of a proverb in a given situation, even when the rationale is explained.

The metaphor of proverb thus functions as a kind of hedge, or a way of aligning and coordinating one's personal view of the world with any given situation. The study of hedges has both psychological and linguistic (see especially Fraser 1980) bases, but essentially delineates the types of linguistic strategies by which one justifies placing persons, objects, or situations into specific categories. For instance, a sentence like *Jack is sort of an atheist* could be used to indicate the speaker's opinion that Jack fulfills certain criteria for being an atheist, although he is not in fact an atheist. The speaker wishes to place Jack into the category of "atheist" and uses the hedge "sort of" to accomplish this. Similar hedges include phrases like "loosely speaking," "technically," and "practically."

Another type of hedge is metaphorical, as when someone says "Ed is a fish." In this case the speaker does not wish (probably) to assert that Ed is in fact an actual fish, assuming that Ed is a human being. He wishes rather to foreground some aspect of Ed, like his drinking habits or swimming ability, by means of comparison. From the example given, one sees that the comparison could have either a positive or negative connotation, depending on the social context in which it is uttered. It is also possible that the characterization of Ed in the metaphorical hedge would not be acceptable to another person for whom the particular characteristic of Ed being discussed did not bear comparison to any characteristic in that person's category of *fish*. That is to say, the criteria for placing a person, object, or situation into any particular category may vary from person to person. This is evidenced in daily life by such differences of opinion as to whether a tomato is a vegetable or a fruit, whether a whale is a fish or a mammal, or whether a certain person resembles a pig in some way. Such opinions are usually supported by both parties involved listing their criteria for "vegetableness," "fishness," or "pigness," and showing how the object being discussed fits their criteria for these categories.

All this is by way of underscoring the fact that the situation, or the aspect of the situation that provokes the use of a proverb may be in some measure idiosyncratic to the user and thus not match the categorization of the same situation by another observer. Thus the categories that a user of a given proverb intends to relate through his use of the proverb may not be related in the same way in another person's cognitive framework, and so may be lost on that person.

CONCLUSION

IN THE PRECEDING PAGES, our goal has been to characterize the riddle as conventional performance. As a means of attaining this end, we have examined representative examples of English language riddles. Our comments, therefore, are tied to a general corpus and should be regarded as suggesting a relatively broad framework for riddle analysis. Certainly the focus and emphasis of any specific repertoire, whether individual or cultural, will vary within the parameters we propose. Despite such adjustments, however, certain patterns prevail.

As licensed artful communication, the act of riddling exploits our expectations concerning utterance and the frameworks generated by prescribed conventions. Thus, various sorts of norms, both utilitarian and ludic, are explored and manipulated. Therefore, as is the case with all cultural behavior, riddling is a system that is intimately connected to other systems; the riddle draws vitality from and revitalizes related contexts.

The contextual system to which we have devoted our most intensive analysis is language. The grammatical structure of the language in which riddles are realized affords rich opportunities for the creation of verbal duplicity. Thus, by discerning the malleable areas of grammar, the riddling tradition of a given group avails participants of the chance to simultaneously play and learn, to grasp both the flexibility and the immutability of language in a single act.

That it is the linguistic code in its entirety which is the issue is reaffirmed by the fact that some riddles exploit relationships between the spoken and the written system of the language. In such instances riddling accommodates a range of the culture's expressive capacities by generating a product in which both our oral and our visual perceptions are called to question.

Similarly, just as riddling forces participants to come to terms with the mechanisms of expression, riddlers and riddlees are drawn into confronting the cognitive foundations of these utterances. As riddle mechanisms appear as a spectrum of techniques, the origins of riddles are similarly diverse. Obviously, those grammatical ambiguities that are incorporated as riddle performances also arise in utilitarian speech contexts as accidents. As such, these strategies are explainable in terms of the formal features of the linguistic system. Conversely, there are riddles that appeal not merely to linguistic but to cognitive frames of reference. This other strategy, though comparable to the grammatically ambiguous mode, entails act rather than accident as a catalyst and impels us to address yet another stratum of the creative process (see Green and Pepicello 1983).

In comprehending riddles, therefore, we encounter a larger sphere of art. Although riddles utilize an intentional overlap of referential frames to derive artful utterances, we discover that they are not unique in this regard. Therefore, we have demonstrated that a similar principle operates in proverbs and in metaphor. Elsewhere we have considered ambiguity as a strategy in folk drama as well (Green and Pepicello, forthcoming). Perhaps, then, the proposition put forth for riddling may suggest useful approaches to other genres of verbal art, also.

Cross-generic applications aside, it seems clear that riddles, far from being no more than an amusing bit of entertainment, are inextricably bound to those most sophisticated of human systems: language, culture, and art. There is nothing novel about this suggestion; we merely echo the sentiments of many of our colleagues (e.g., Abrahams 1980, McDowell 1979, Sutton-Smith 1976). We do hope, however, that the notions we have advanced will assist in the continued exploration of the means by which structure and license, sense and nonsense converge in the traditional riddle.

POSTSCRIPT: A CROSS-CULTURAL APPLICATION

IT IS NOT OUR intention to present a cross-cultural survey of riddle strategies; however, it is useful at this point to ask whether the framework we have proposed functions beyond the English data we have analyzed. By way of partially answering this question, we have examined approximately three hundred Spanish riddles from several riddling traditions.[1] The results of our examination have tended to support our framework as a viable classificatory tool in several ways that we shall now discuss.

First, we found that Spanish riddles, as with the English riddles treated, employ strategies at the levels of phonology, morphology, and syntax. The highly inflectional nature of Spanish riddles results in differences at each level that merit discussion. At the phonological level, we find lexical ambiguity of the type we have discussed in riddles like 1.

1.	Siempre dice algo	It always says something
	y no sabe hablar;	and it doesn't know how to talk;
	Puede correr	It can run
	pero nunca caminar	but never walk.
	¿Qué es? *El reloj.*	What is it? *A watch.*

Here the words *dice* 'says' and *correr* 'to run' manifest the same ambiguity as regards reference to time or to human activity as their English counterparts, and the wit of the riddle turns on this ambiguity.

A number of Spanish riddles combine lexical ambiguity with the contrast between masculine and feminine gender forms of a given word, as in 2–4.

2. ¿Qué es lo que hace el pato con la pata? *El nido.*
   What does a (male) duck make with his foot/a female duck? *A nest.*
3. ¿Qué animal anda con una pata? *Un pato.*
   What animal walks with his foot/a female duck? *A (male) duck.*
4. ¿Cuál es el animal que lleva la hembra en la barba? *El chivo.*
   What animal carries its female in his beard? *A goat* (feminine *chiva* also means "goatee").

In 2 and 3 the ambiguity is straightforward. In these cases there is insufficient context to distinguish whether *pata* means 'foot' or 'female duck,' and the ambiguity is resolved only when the answer is revealed. In 4 the strategy varies slightly, wherein the answer, *chivo*, is the masculine form of the word for 'goat.' Once the answer is revealed, it requires the riddlee to call forth the feminine counterpart *chiva*, which exhibits the ambiguity upon which the wit of the riddle turns.

Still at the phonological level, we find riddles that exploit stress and juncture in creating a block element, as in 5.

5. Oro parece, plata no es
   Quien no lo adivina
   Bien tonto es
   Ya te he lo dicho. *El plátano.*
   It seems to be gold, it is not silver/it is a banana
   Whoever doesn't get it
   Is quite foolish
   I just told you the answer. *A banana.*

Here the crucial element is the placement of stress and juncture within a string of phonemes, yielding either /plata + noes/ 'it is not silver' or /plátano + es/ 'it is a banana.' In the flow of normal speech, this difference is easily neutralized, and the former reading is reinforced by the word *oro*, 'gold.' The solution then draws attention to the crucial phonological factors.

As with all stress and juncture-related riddles, the phonological shifts under discussion entail different syntactic analyses, as well. This same phonological/syntactic strategy is seen in 6.

6. Espera amiga porque
   Espera te digo si no me
   lo adivinas no te vas conmigo. *Pera.*
   Wait my friend because
   I tell you to wait; if you don't
   Guess it you aren't going with me.
   or
   It is a pear, my friend, because
   I tell you it is a pear; if you don't
   guess it, you aren't going with me. *A pear.*

Here we find contrastive play between /espera/ 'wait' and /es + pera/ 'it is a pear,' whereby the crucial use of juncture is again submerged by the rapidity of normal speech. In addition, as also in 5, the solution is obscured by the fact that the riddlee is not attuned to discern the answer to the riddle within the riddle question itself. It is important to note that riddles like 5 and 6, as was the case with many English riddles, must be orally transmitted to be effective, since their written form becomes cumbersome.

At the morphological level, we find again several strategies that are directly related to those we have outlined for English riddles. The most closely related strategy involves the exploitation of pseudomorphemes, as in 7 and 8.

7. Agua pasa por mi casa
   cate de mi corazon. *Aguacate.*
   Water passes through my house
   Watch out for my heart. *Avocado.*
8. ¿Cuál es la planta
   que hay que decir algo
   para después darle el don? *Algodón.*
   What is the plant
   to which one must say something
   so that it later gives you a gift? *Cotton.*

One point to be made about riddles like these is that although they turn on pseudomorphemes, the overall riddle strategy is not the same as English riddles that utilize pseudomorphemes. In English riddles like "What room can no one enter? A mushroom" the pseudomorpheme appears in the question and is revealed as such in the answer. In the Spanish riddles 7 and 8, the two pseudomorphemes involved in each appear as free morphemes in what appears to be a riddle metaphor. The riddlee's task is to discern which free morphemes in the riddle question may be combined to provide an apt referent for the description in the question.

Thus, in 7 we have a metaphorical description of an avocado. The morphemes *agua*, 'water,' and *cate*, 'watch out,' appear in the metaphorical description and are combined in the answer *aguacate*, although they do not function as morphemes of this word. In 8 this strategy is intensified in that the answer *algodón*, 'cotton,' is not an apparent referent in view of the riddle question. Rather, the question seems to be merely a vehicle for the presentation of the morphemes *algo*, 'something,' and *don*, 'gift,' which are then employed as pseudomorphemes. This strategy is noted by Beutler 1979 as a frequent one in certain areas of Mexico.

A second morphological strategy is seen in riddles like 9.

9. ¿Cuándo se convierte una canción en un golpe duro?
Cuando canto se convierte en cantazo.
When is a song changed into a hard blow with a rock?
When the word canto (song or rock) is changed into cantazo (a hard blow with a rock).

The strategy here is in fact double. First there is a play made on the word *canto*, which may mean either 'song' or 'rock.' The former reading is focused upon by the unambiguous use of *canción*, 'song,' in the riddle question. Secondly, the derivational suffix *-azo* is employed to complete the solution, in that *-azo* designates a blow executed with the noun stem to which it is attached, in this case *cant-* 'rock,' giving 'blow with a rock.' Thus lexical ambiguity provides the environment for morphological manipulation in this riddle.

We have noted above that syntactic strategies are closely related to phonological ones, especially to stress- and juncture-related strategies, in the riddles examined. One riddle encountered plays upon phonology, morphology, and syntax to produce what Hockett 1977 calls an 'imperfect pun':

10. ¿En qué se parece una cama a un elefante?
El uno es paquidermo, la otra es pa'que duerma.
How is a bedroom like an elephant?
One is a pachiderm (paquidermo), the other is for sleeping (pa'que duerma).

The primary phonological strategy here is contraction, whereby the sequence *para que duerma*, 'for sleeping,' becomes *pa'que duerma* (/para ke dwerma/→/pake dwerma/). This renders this syntactic construction identical with *paquidermo* /pakidermo/, save for the second vowel and the additional /w/ in the former. This strategy closely resembles the English exploitation of minimal pairs.

At the morphological level we find that the riddle question asks for a comparison of, among other things, a feminine noun (*la cama*) with a masculine one (*el elefante*). In the answer the syntactic unit *pa'que duerma*, which is being contrasted with the simple noun *paquidermo* gives the appearance of a feminine noun, i.e., it ends in *-a*, as one would expect given the dichotomy set up in the riddle question. Finally, at the syntactic level, we find that the contraction of *para que duerma* renders this syntactic unit comparable to the simple noun *paquidermo* and thus produces the wit on which the riddle turns. This strategy is similar to that of the English riddle "Why is a mouse like the grass? Because the cat'll (cattle) eat it."

Thus we find that Spanish riddles employ a variety of linguistic strategies that closely parallel those outlined for English riddles. The same is true if we consider metaphorically-based riddles like 11–13:

11. Soy delgada y amarilla	I am thin and yellow
con pelo coloradito	with reddish hair
si me dejas mucho viva	If you let me live much,

	me derrito despacito	I'll melt very slowly.
	¿Qué es? *La vela.*	What is it? *A candle.*
12.	Verde es su nacimiento	It's green at birth
	Amarillo es su vivir	It's yellow during its life
	Negro se va poniendo	And it turns black
	Cuando se que quiere morir	When it's ready to die
	Adivina lo que es.	Guess what it is.
	El plátano.	*A banana.*
13.	Riye como el león	It roars like a lion
	Y escarba como el peon	And digs like a peasant
	Adivina lo que es.	Guess what is is.
	La cascada.	*A waterfall.*

Although these riddles are clearly metaphorical, we also find some that, as was the case in English, exhibit elements of both grammatical and metaphorical ambiguity, but that fit neither category exactly. Consider, for example, 14:

14.	Dos niñas en un balcón	Two girls/pupils on a balcony
	Bailando al mismo son,	dancing to the same music
	¿Qué son? *Los ojos.*	What are they? *Eyes.*

Here we find the metaphorical comparison of the coordinated movement of the human eyes to a pair of dancing girls on a balcony, i.e., in the sockets under the overhand of the brow. However, the word *niñas* may mean "pupil" (of the eye) as well as "girl," so that the riddle may be taken as a more literal description, one containing a crucial lexical ambiguity. Thus both types of ambiguity are in play in 14.

Finally, we note the use of sight/spelling riddles in Spanish. These riddles are on the whole more elaborate than their English counterparts, as seen in 16 and 17, although some, like 15, are more closely related to the English-based strategy.

15. Estoy in medio del río	I'm in the middle of the river
ni me mojo ni tengo frío	I'm neither wet nor cold
¿Quién soy? *La letra 'i'.*	Who am I? *The letter 'i'.*
16. En el medio del mar estoy	I'm in the middle of the ocean
no soy astro ni estrella	I'm neither heavenly body nor star
ni tampoco luna bella	nor lovely moon.
Adivina lo que soy	Guess what I am
No soy de dios ni del mundo	I'm not of God nor of the world
ni del infierno profundo	nor of deep hell
En medio del mar estoy.	I'm in the middle of the ocean.
La letra 'a'.	*The letter 'a'.*
17. Soy la redondez del mundo	I'm the roundness of the world
sin me no puede habe Dios;	without me there would be no God.
papas y cardenales, sí,	A pope and cardinals, yes,
pero pontífice no.	but no pontiff.
La letra 'o'.	*The letter 'o'.*

In 15 and 16 we see fairly straightforward strategies of the types discussed previously. Riddle 17 combines two strategies, playing upon shape ('roundness of the world' referring to the shape of the *o* in *mundo*), as well as the spelling of various words containing *o*. In all cases, however, these riddles deal with the written code and use the conventions of this code in creating a block element.

1. Beutler 1979, Morillo 1974, Varricchio 1980, R. King 1981, P. King 1981.

APPENDIX: THE RIDDLES

1. The following riddles were taken from Archer Taylor 1951. The numbers enclosed in parentheses following the riddles are those assigned by Taylor.

Many eyes and never a nose, one tongue, and about it goes. *Shoe.* (14)

What's this that's got a heart in its head? *Lettuce.* (31)

There is something with a heart in its head. *Peach.* (33)

It first walks on four legs, then on two, then on three legs. *Man.* (46b)

What has an eye,/But cannot see? *Needle.* (282)

What has a tongue and can't talk? *Shoe.* (296a)

What has teeth but cannot eat? *Saw.* (298)

What has teeth but does not eat? *Comb.* (299)

White bird featherless/Flew from Paradise,/Perched upon the castle wall;/Up came Lord John landless,/Took it up handless,/And rode away horseless/To the King's white hall. *Snow.* (368)

I have a cock on yonder hill,/I keep him for a wonder,/And every time the cock do crow,/It lightens, hails, and thunders. *A gun.* (380)

Two legs sat on three legs./Up jumped four legs/And grabs one leg. *Man sitting on a three-legged stool; up jump a dog and grabs ham on the table.* (461d)

In spring I am gay,/In handsome array;/In summer more clothing I wear;/When colder it grows,/I fling off my clothes,/And in winter I quite naked appear. *A tree.* (587b)

Blackey went into blackey, blackey came out of blackey, and blackey left whitey in blackey. *A black hen went in a black stump and laid a white egg.* (867)

Black and white and red all over. *Newspaper* (1498a)

A house full, a yard full,/Couldn't catch a bowl full. *Smoke.* (1643a)

2. The following examples were drawn from Coffin and Cohen 1974. Page numbers are indicated in parentheses following each text.

What is the best butter on earth? *A goat.* (144)

What is the difference between a pretty girl and a mouse? *One charms the he's, and the other harms the cheese.* (147)

What is the difference between a jeweler and a jailer? *One sells watches and the other watches cells.* (147)

What has teeth but can't eat? *A comb.* (143)

3. The next text was taken from Abrahams and Dundes 1972. The page number is indicated in parentheses.

Crooked and straight, which way are you going? Croptail every year, what makes you care? *Meadow to a brook and the brook's reply.* (135)

4. The following riddle was collected in Georgia in 1977 by David Stanley from an 85-year-old informant.

White comes out of white, and run white out of white. *A white dog runs out of a white house and chases a white cow out of a cotton patch.*

5. The following riddle is taken from Maranda 1971a. The page number is indicated in parentheses.

What tree grows without roots? *Human being.* (119)

6. The following riddle is taken from McDowell 1979. The page number is indicated in parentheses.

The tree has only two leaves, what is it? *A man and his ears.* (247)

7. The final set of riddles in our corpus are those we have collected from 1976–81. The majority of examples were provided by colleagues and students at the University of Delaware, Temple University, and Texas A&M University. Additional riddles were recorded at a brief riddle session between two seven-year-old children, and the remainder were provided by audience members who approached us after paper presentations at professional meetings. The majority of these riddles were presented to us more than once, and many of these texts are variants of riddles published in scholarly collections. Thus, we feel safe in assuming that they constitute a reasonable sampling of contemporary American riddles in the English language.

What has a mouth but cannot eat? *River.*
What has an eye that never closes? *Needle.*
What bird is in the lowest spirits? *Bluebird.*
What weapon does an angry lover resemble? *Crossbow.*
When is a black dog not a black dog? *When it is a greyhound.*
Why is a man clearing a hedge in a single bound like a man snoring? *He does it in his sleep (his leap).*
When is it hard to get your watch out of your pocket? *When it keeps sticking (keeps ticking) there.*
What is the difference between a baby and a coat? *One you wear, one you were.*
What is the difference between a ballet dancer and a duck? *One goes quick on her legs, the other goes quack on her legs.*
Why is coffee like the soil? *It is ground.*
When is a rope like a child at school? *When taut (taught).*
When is a doctor most annoyed? *When he is out of patients (patience).*
What musical instrument should one not believe? *A lyre (liar).*
What kind of bow can you never tie? *A rainbow.*
What kind of ears does a train have? *Engineers.*
What room can no one enter? *A mushroom.*
What driver is never arrested? *A screwdriver.*

On what side of a country church is the graveyard? *The outside.*
What miss is most unpopular? *Misfortune.*
What ship has two mates but no captain? *Courtship.*
What is the key to a good dinner? *Turkey.*
What chins are never shaved? *Urchins.*
What pets make the sweetest music? *Trumpets.*
What kind of cat do you find in the library? *Catalogue.*
What are the biggest kind of ants? *Giants.*
What is the gentlest kind of spur? *Whisper.*
Why is a goose/duck like an icicle? *Both grow down.*
When is a boy like a pony? *When he is a little horse.*
What do you call a man who marries another man? *A minister.*
Would you rather have an elephant kill you or a gorilla? *I'd rather have the elephant kill the gorilla.*
When is a man like a snake? *When he is rattled.*
When is a lamp in bad humor? *When it is put out.*
What does a person grow if he works hard in his garden? *Tired.*
What goes most against a farmer's grain? *A reaper.*
What flowers does a person always carry? *Tulips (two lips).*
When is a boat like a heap of snow? *When it is adrift.*
Why is a fish dealer never generous? *His business makes him sell fish (selfish).*
Why is a mouse like grass? *The cattle (cat'll) eat it.*
Why can't you starve to death in the desert? *Because of the sandwiches (sand which is) there.*
What is the difference between a deer fleeing from hunters and a midget witch? *One is hunted stag, the other a stunted hag.*
What is the difference between a professional musician and one who hears him? *One plays for his pay, the other pays for his play.*
What is the difference between a donkey and a postage stamp? *One you lick with a stick, the other you stick with a lick.*
What is the difference between a sewing machine and a kiss? *One sews seams nice, the other seems so nice.*

What is the difference between a hungry man and a glutton? *One longs to eat, the other eats too long.*
What makes a road broad? *The letter B.*
What do the letters x,p,d,n, and c spell? *Expediency.*
Spell enemy in three letters. *NME.*
What are the most sensible letters? *Y's (wise).*
What letters are most provoking? *T's (tease).*
How many P's (peas) are in a pint? *One.*
What is the end of everything? *G.*
What changes a lad into a lady? *Y.*
What changes a pear into a pearl? *L.*
What occurs twice in a moment, once in a minute, and never in a thousand years? *M.*
What part of London is in France? *N.*
What tune does everyone know? *Fortune.*
What age is served at breakfast? *Sausage.*
What state is round at both ends and high in the middle? *Ohio.*
What plant stands for the number four? *IV (ivy).*
What must you add to nine to make it six? *S (IX).*
Add ten to nothing and what animal does it make? *OX.*
Why is the number nine like a peacock? *Remove its tail and it is nothing.*
Where is the smallest bridge in the world? *On your nose.*
What has a bed but never sleeps? *A river.*
What lock can no key open? *A lock of hair.*
What vegetable is unpopular on ships? *A leek.*
When did Moses sleep five in a bed? *When he slept with his forefathers.*
What toe never gets a corn? *Mistletoe.*

BIBLIOGRAPHY

Abrahams, Roger D. 1968.
"Introductory Remarks to a Rhetorical Theory of Folklore." *Journal of American Folklore* 81:143–58.

_______ 1972.
The Literary Study of the Riddle." *Texas Studies in Literature and Language* 14:177–97.

_______ 1973.
"Ritual for fun and profit, or the ends and outs of celebration." Paper delivered to Burg Wartenstein Symposium #59.

_______ 1976.
"The Complex Relations of Simple Forms," in Dan Ben-Amos, ed., *Folklore Genres*. Austin: University of Texas Press.

_______ 1980.
Between the Living and the Dead. Helsinki: Academia Scientarum Fennica.

_______ 1981.
"In and Out of Performance." *Narodna umjetnost* 1. 69–78.

Abrahams, Roger D. and Alan Dundes.
"Riddles," in Dorson 1972.

Arewa, E. Ojo and Alan Dundes 1964.
"Proverbs and the Ethnography of Speaking." *American Anthropologist* 66, pt. 2. 70–85.

Aristotle.
The Poetics.

Aronoff, Mark 1980.
"Contextuals." *Language* 56:744–58.

Austerlitz, Robert 1960.
"Parallelismus," in *Poetics, Poetyka, поэтика*. The Hague: Mouton.

Austin, J. L. 1970.
Philosophical Papers. London: Oxford University Press.

Babcock-Abrahams, Barbara 1974.
"The Story in the Story: Metanarration in Folk Narrative." Paper delivered at the sixth Folk Narrative Congress, Helsinki, Finland.

Barthes, Roland 1964.
Elements de semiologie. Paris: Seuil.

Bascom, William R. 1949.
"Literary Style in Yoruba Riddles." *Journal of American Folklore* 62:1-16.

Bateson, Gregory 1972.
Steps to an Ecology of Mind. New York: Ballantine.

Bauman, Richard 1975.
"Verbal Art as Performance." *American Anthropologist* 77:290-311.

Ben-Amos, Dan 1971.
"Toward a Definition of Folklore in Context." *Journal of American Folklore* 84:3-15.

——— 1976.
"Solutions to Riddles." *Journal of American Folklore* 89:249-54.

Beutler, Gisela 1979.
Adivinanzas Españolas de la Tradicion Popular Actual de Mexico, Principalmente de las Regiones de Puebla-Tlaxcala. Wiesbaden: Franz Steiner Verlag.

Bickerton, Derek 1969.
"Prolegomena to a linguistic theory of metaphor." *Foundations of Language* 5:34-52.

Burke, Kenneth 1941.
The Philosophy of Literary Form. Baton Rouge: Louisiana State University Press.

——— 1968.
Counter-Statement. Los Angeles: University of California Press.

——— 1969.
A Grammar of Motives. Los Angeles: University of California Press.

Burns, Elizabeth 1972.
Theatricality: A Study of Convention in the Theatre and in Social Life. London: Longman.

Burns, Thomas A. 1976.
"Riddling: Occasion to Act." *Journal of American Folklore* 89:139-65.

Chomsky, Noam 1957.
Syntactic Structures. The Hague: Mouton.

——— 1965.
Aspects of the Theory of Syntax. Cambridge, Mass.: MIT Press.

Clark, Eve and Herbert Clark 1979.
"When nouns surface as verbs." *Language* 55:767-811.

Coffin, Tristam and Hennig Cohen, eds., 1974.
Folklore and the Working Folk of America. New York: Anchor Press.

Crowley, Daniel J. 1966.
I Could Talk Old Story Good. Los Angeles: University of California Press.

Darnell, Regna 1974.
"Correlates of Cree Narrative Performance," in Richard Bauman and Joel Sherzer, eds., *Explorations in the Ethnography of Speaking*. New York: Cambridge University Press.

de Saussure, Ferdinand 1922.
Cours de linguistique generale. Paris: Champion.

Dorson, Richard, ed. 1972.
Folklore and Folklife: An Introduction. Chicago: University of Chicago Press.

Dundes, Alan 1964.
"Texture, Text, and Context." *Southern Folklore Quarterly* 28:251-65.

_______ 1975.
"On the Structure of the Proverb." *Proverbium* 25.961-73.

Edie, James 1976.
Speaking and Meaning: The Phenomenology of Language. Bloomington: Indiana University Press.

Empson, William 1947.
Seven Types of Ambiguity. Toronto: Oxford Press.

Evans, David 1976.
"Riddling and the Structure of Context." *Journal of American Folklore* 89:166-88.

Firth, Raymond 1926.
"Proverbs in Native Life, with Special Reference to those of the Maori." *Folk-Lore* 37:134-53, 245-70.

Fox, James 1974.
"Our Ancestors Spoke in Pairs," in Richard Bauman and Joel Sherzer, eds., *Explorations in the Ethnography of Speaking*. New York: Cambridge University Press.

Francis, W. Nelson 1958.
The Structure of American English. New York: The Ronald Press Company.

Fraser, Bruce 1980.
"The Interpretation of Novel Metaphors," in Andrew Ortony, ed., *Metaphor and Thought*. London: Cambridge University Press.

Gardner, Howard, Ellen Winner, R. Bechofer, D. Wolf 1978.
"The Development of Figurative Language," in Keith E. Nelson, ed., *Children's Language Volume 1*. New York: Gardner Press.

Geertz, Clifford 1980.
"Blurred Genres: The Refiguration of Social Thought." *Scholar* 49:165-79.

Georges, Robert A. 1969.
"Toward an Understanding of Storytelling Events." *Journal of American Folklore* 82:313-28.

Georges, Robert A. and Alan Dundes 1963.
"Toward a Structural Definition of the Riddle." *Journal of American Folklore* 76:111-18.

Glazier, Jack and Phyllis G. Glazier 1976.
"Ambiguity and Exchange: The Double Dimension of Mbeere Riddles." *Journal of American Folklore* 89:189–238.

Goffman, Erving 1974.
Frame Analysis: An Essay on the Organization of Experience. New York: Harper and Row.

Gossen, Gary 1972.
"Chamula Genres of Verbal Behavior," in Americo Paredes and Richard Bauman, eds., *Toward New Perspectives in Folklore.* Austin: University of Texas Press.

_______ 1974.
"To Speak with a Heated Heart: Chamula Canons of Style and Good Performance," in Richard Bauman and Joel Sherzer, eds., *Explorations in the Ethnography of Speaking.* New York: Cambridge University Press.

Green, Thomas A. and W. J. Pepicello 1978.
"Wit in Riddling: A Linguistic Perspective." *Genre* 11:1–13.

_______ 1979.
"The Folk Riddle: A Redefinition of Terms." *Western Folklore* 38:3–20.

_______ 1980.
"Sight and Spelling Riddles." *Journal of American Folklore* 93:23–34.

_______ 1983.
"The Riddle Process." *Journal of American Folklore*, forthcoming.

_______ 1984.
"The Semiotics of Puppetry." *Semiotica*, forthcoming.

Guiraud, Pierre 1971.
La Semiologie. Paris: Presses Universitaires de France.

Hamnett, Ian 1967.
"Ambiguity, Classification and Change: The Function of Riddles." *Man* 2:379–92.

Haring, Lee 1974.
"On Knowing the Answer." *Journal of American Folklore* 87:197–207.

Harries, Lyndon 1971.
"The Riddle in Africa." *Journal of American Folklore* 84:377–93.

Hockett, Charles 1977.
The View From Language. Athens: University of Georgia Press.

Hymes, Dell 1970.
"The Ethnography of Speaking," in Thomas Gladwin and William C. Sturtevant, eds., *Anthropology and Human Behavior.* Washington, D.C.: The Anthropological Society of Washington.

_______ 1975.
"Breakthrough into Performance," in Dan Ben-Amos and Kenneth Goldstein, eds., *Folklore: Performance and Communication.* The Hague: Mouton.

Innes, Gordon 1974.
Sunjata: Three Mandinka Versons. London: School of Oriental and African Studies.

Jakobson, Roman 1966.
"Grammatical Parallelism and its Russian Facet." *Language* 42:399–429.

——— 1968.
"Poetry of Grammar and Grammar of Poetry." *Lingua* 21:597–609.

——— 1971.
"Two Aspects of Language and Two Types of Aphasic Disturbances," in *Selected Writings II*. The Hague: Mouton.

Jansen, William H. 1957.
"Classifying Performance in the Study of Verbal Folklore," in W. Edson Richmond, ed., *Studies in Folklore*. Bloomington: Indiana University Press.

Jones, Bessie and Bess Lomax Hawes 1972.
Step It Down: Games, Plays, Songs, and Stories from the Afro-American Heritage. New York: Harper and Row.

Karchevsky, S. 1929.
"Du dualisme asymetrique du signe linguistique." *Travaux du Cercle Linguistique de Prague* 1:33–38.

Katz, J. J. and J. A. Fodor 1963.
"The Structure of a Semantic Theory." *Language* 39:170–210.

Keenan, Elinor 1973.
"A Sliding Sense of Obligatoriness: The Poly-Structure of Malagasy Oratory." *Language in Society* 2:225–43.

——— 1974.
"Norm Makers, Norm Breakers: Uses of Speech by Men and Women in a Malagasy Community," in Richard Bauman and Joel Sherzer, eds., *Explorations in the Ethnography of Speaking*. New York: Cambridge University Press.

King, D. Robert 1981.
"An Investigation of the Riddle Form in Spanish." Unpublished manuscript.

King, Patricia 1981.
"Riddles in Spanish." Unpublished manuscript.

Layton, Monique J. 1976.
"Luba and Finnish Riddles: A Double Analysis." *Journal of American Folklore* 89:239–48.

Leech, Geoffrey 1966.
"Linguistics and the figures of rhetoric," in Roger Fowler, ed., *Essays on Style and Language*. London: Routledge and Kegan Paul.

Levin, J. I. 1977.
"The Structure of Metaphor," in Daniel P. Lucid, ed., *Soviet Semiotics*. Baltimore: The Johns Hopkins University Press.

Levin, S. R. 1977.
The Semantics of Metaphor. Baltimore: The Johns Hopkins University Press.

Lieber, Michael 1976.
"Riddles, Cultural Categories, and World View." *Journal of American Folklore* 89:255–65.

Lomax, Alan 1968.
Folk Song Style and Culture. Washington, D.C.: American Association for the Advancement of Science.

Lord, Albert B. 1960.
The Singer of Tales. Cambridge, Mass.: Harvard University Press.

Lotman, Ju. M. 1970.
"Two Models of Communication," *Theses of the Reports at the Fourth Summer School on Secondary Modeling Systems*. Tartu: Tartu University.

Lucid, Daniel P., ed., 1977.
Soviet Semiotics. Baltimore: The Johns Hopkins University Press.

Lyons, John 1969.
Introduction to Theoretical Linguistics. Cambridge: University of Cambridge Press.

Maranda, Elli Köngäs 1971.
"The Logic of Riddles," in Pierre Maranda and Elli Köngäs Maranda, eds., *Structural Analysis of Oral Tradition*. Philadelphia: University of Pennsylvania Press.

_______ 1971a.
"A Tree Grows: Transformations of a Riddle Metaphor," in *Structural Models in Folklore and Transformational Essays*, Pierre Maranda and Elli Köngäs Maranda. The Hague: Mouton.

_______ 1971b.
"Theory and Practice of Riddle Analysis," *Journal of American Folklore* 84: 51-61.

_______, ed. 1976.
Riddles and Riddling. Special issue of *Journal of American Folklore*, 89.

McDowell, John 1974.
"Some Aspects of Verbal Art in Bolivian Quechua." *Folklore Annual of the University Folklore Association*. no. 6: University of Texas at Austin.

_______ 1979.
Children's Riddling. Bloomington: Indiana University Press.

Meier, John 1901.
Grundis der germanischen Philologie. Strassburg.

Mooij, J. J. A. 1976.
A Study of Metaphor. Amsterdam: North Holland.

Morillo, Jane 1974.
Riddles from Venezuela. Unpublished manuscript.

Nida, Eugene 1948.
"The Identification of Morphemes." *Language* 24:414–41.

Novakovic, Stojan 1877.
Srpske Narodne zagonetke. Panchevo.

Ortony, Andrew, ed., 1980.
Metaphor and Thought. Cambridge: Cambridge University Press.

Pepicello, W. J. 1980.
"Linguistic Strategies in Riddling." *Western Folklore* 39: 1–16.

Petsch, Robert 1899.
Neue Beitrage zur Kenntnis des Volksratsels, Palaestra IV. Berlin.

Plato, *Kratylos*.

Propp, V. 1968.
Morphology of the Folktale, trans. L. Scott. Austin: University of Texas Press.

Reaver, J. Russell 1972.
"From Reality to Fantasy: Opening-Closing Formulas in the Structures of American Tall Tales." *Southern Folklore Quarterly* 36:369–82.

Roche, M. 1973.
Phenomenology, Language, and the Social Sciences. London: Routledge and Kegan Paul.

Rosaldo, Michelle Z. 1973.
"I Have Nothing to Hide: The Language of Ilongot Oratory." *Language in Society* 2:193–233.

Rosie, A. M. 1973.
Information and Communication Theory. London: Van Nostrand Reinhold Co.

Sapir, J. David 1970.
"The Anatomy of Metaphor," in J. D. Sapir and J. C. Crocker, eds., *The Social Use of Metaphor: Essays on the Anthropology of Rhetoric* (Philadelphia: University of Pennsylvania Press).

Scott, Charles 1965.
Persian and Arabic Riddles: A Language-Centered Approach to Genre Definition. Bloomington: Indiana University and Mouton.

——— 1969.
"On Defining the Riddle: The Problem of a Structural Unit." *Genre* 2:129–42.

Seitel, Peter 1976.
"Proverbs: A Social Use of Metaphor," in Dan Ben-Amos, ed., *Folklore Genres*. Austin: University of Texas Press.

Sherzer, Dina and Joel Sherzer 1972.
"Literature in San Blas: Discovering the Cuna *Ikala*." *Semiotica* 6:182–99.

Sherzer, Joel 1974.
"Namakke, sunakke, Kormakke: Three Types of Cuna Speech Events," in Richard Bauman and Joel Sherzer, eds., *Explorations in the Ethnography of Speaking*. New York: Cambridge University Press.

Stankiewicz, Edward 1960.
"Poetic Language and Non-Poetic Language in their Interrelation," in *Poetics, Poetyka,* поэтика . The Hague: Mouton.

Stanley, David 1977.
"Georgia Project Notes." Unpublished manuscript.

Sutton-Smith, Brian 1976.

"A Developmental Structural Account of Riddles," in B. Kirshenblatt-Gimblett, ed., *Speech Play: Research and Resource for the Study of Linguistic Creativity*. Philadelphia: University of Pennsylvania Press.

Taylor, Archer 1931.
The Proverb. Cambridge, Mass.: Harvard University Press.

_______ 1943.
"The Riddle." *California Folklore Quarterly* 2:129–47.

_______ 1951.
English Riddles from Oral Tradition. Los Angeles: University of California Press.

Tedlock, Dennis 1972.
"On the Translation of Style in Oral Narrative," in Americo Paredes and Richard Bauman, eds., *Toward New Perspectives in Folklore*. Austin: University of Texas Press.

Thomas, Owen 1969.
Metaphor and Related Subjects. New York: Random House.

Toelken, J. Barre 1969.
"The 'Pretty Language' of Yellowman: Genre, Mode, and Texture in Navaho Coyote Narratives." *Genre* 2:211–35.

Uspensky, B. A. 1972.
"Structural Isomorphism of Verbal and Visual Art." *Poetics* 5:5–39.

_______ 1977.
"Semiotics of Art," in Daniel P. Lucid, ed., *Soviet Semiotics*. Baltimore: The Johns Hopkins Press.

Vachek, Josef 1970.
The Linguistic School of Prague. Bloomington: Indiana University Press.

Varricchio, Andrea 1980.
"Spanish Riddles.' Unpublished manuscript.

Zug, Charles 1967.
"The Nonrational Riddle: The Zen Koan." *Journal of American Folklore* 80:81–88.

INDEX

CPSIA information can be obtained
at www.ICGtesting.com
Printed in the USA
LVHW091619120821
694757LV00011B/66

9 780814 253458